# Successful
## Investing Formulas

Lucile Tomlinson

Published by Snowball Publishing

Cover Design: J.Neuman

**www.snowballpublishing.com**

**info@snowballpublishing.com**

For information regarding special discounts for bulk purchases, please contact
Snowball Publishing at

sales@snowballpublishing.com

# PREFACE

The New York Stock Exchange has put considerable effort into popularizing its "monthly purchase plan," under which an investor devotes the same dollar amount each month to buying one or more common stocks. This is an application of a special type of "formula investment" known as dollar-cost averaging. During the predominantly rising-market experience since 1949 the results from such a procedure were certain to be highly satisfactory, especially since they prevented the practitioner from concentrating his buying at the wrong times. In Lucile Tomlinson's comprehensive study, the author presented a calculation of the results of dollar-cost averaging in the group of stocks making up the Dow Jones industrial index. Tests were made covering 23 ten-year purchase periods...Every test showed a profit either at the close of the purchase period or within five years thereafter. The average indicated profit at the end of the 23 buying periods was 21.5%, exclusive of dividends received.

Needless to say, in some instances there was a substantial temporary depreciation at market value. Miss Tomlinson ends her discussion of this ultrasimple investment formula with the striking sentence: "No one has yet discovered any other formula for investing which can be used with so much confidence of ultimate success, regardless of what may happen to security prices, as Dollar Cost Averaging." It may be objected that dollar-cost averaging, while sound in principle, is rather unrealistic in practice, because few people are so situated that they can have available for common-stock investment the same amount of money each year for, say, 20 years. It seems to me that this apparent objection has lost much of its force in recent years.

Common stocks are becoming generally accepted as a necessary component of a sound savings-investment program. Thus, systematic and uniform purchases of common stocks may present no more psychological and financial difficulties than similar continuous payments for United States savings bonds and for life insurance--to which they should be complementary. The monthly amount may be small, but the results after 20 or more years can be impressive and important to the saver.

**Benjamin Graham**
**The Intelligent Investor.**

**To B.W.T.**

# FOREWORD

HERE is a book of which it can truly be said that the cost of not reading it may be beyond your means. All you have to ask yourself to decide that point in advance is whether you are satisfied with your investment record; or whether you recall with a shudder the times you have bought securities near the highs of their cyclical price ranges, or sold some near the lows.

Formula plans are to investor's emotions what governors are to engines—devices to keep both from running away with themselves. Bull markets result when avarice overcomes fear. Bear markets come about when conditions are the opposite. Formula plans in one way or another compel their adherents to act on the principle that half a loaf is better than no bread *before* the dominant speculative emotion changes.

Some of the investment programs described in this book are complicated, but the underlying philosophy of all of them is summed up in the advice, "When you own so many stocks you can't sleep, sell to the sleeping point," and vice versa. All formula plans have this in common: They are aimed to keep your portfolio in such shape that you literally do not care whether the market goes up or down, because in the long run you will make money either way if the market just continues to fluctuate.

As to the author, seldom is a book written by anyone on any subject with less reason to wonder whether someone else might have been better qualified to do the job. Any idea that finance is only a man's field has been dead longer than Hetty Green, of course. Any thought that older heads might contain more knowledge of the subject than Miss Tomlinson's—whose college education began at Mount Holyoke in 1929—runs bang into the fact that formula planning, like the helicopter, for example, is so new that its pioneers can be young.

For more than ten years, as an associate editor of *Barron's*, as an officer of the National Association of Investment Companies and as a consultant in the field of investment trusts and investment programming, Miss Tomlinson has been acquiring that intimate knowledge of specific facts which brings practical value to the generalizations derived therefrom. The results are set forth in SUCCESSFUL INVESTING FORMULAS.

No special pleading mars the book for those seeking a reference work in this little documented field. With her reportorial abilities for digging up facts and presenting them clearly, Miss Tomlinson combines an all too rare judicial attitude which recognizes that each variety of formula plan has both its own peculiar advantages and disadvantages.

More remarkable in one who has chosen to write a book on the subject, she even can see that in individual instances there are pros and cons to the proposition of using any formula at all, as compared with employing a combination of eternal vigilance and seasoned judgment. The book will appeal most to those who se attempts to fly through stock market fogs by the feeling in the seat of their pants have resulted more often than not in painful contacts with the rocky crags of the unforeseen and unforeseeable.

THOMAS W. PHELPS
Editor *Barron's* 1936–1938

# CONTENTS

# PREFACE

FOR PRACTICAL purposes, this book is a sequel to a series of articles which were published under the same title in *Barron's* in the summer of 1943. While it started out to be a simple revision of those articles, the final result is sufficiently different to require a brief explanation.

The three basic types of formula plans described are the same as were included in the original articles. The changes in details and application are the result of the four years' additional experience which formula planners have had in the practical operation of investment funds and of new research into the subject by the growing number of interested institutional investors.

Few of the plans described in the book are original. I have depended heavily upon the contributions of numerous individuals and organizations whose familiarity with both the problems of investing and the finer points of formula planning, in theory and practice, is far greater than my own. To all of them I am greatly indebted. This book would have been impossible without the helpful suggestions and ideas of so many individuals that it is impracticable to attempt to list them by name. I do, however, wish to express particularly my very deep appreciation to all of the institutions and other organizations who gave me permission to publish the details of their investment plans.

Interest in formula planning is found among all types of investors, from the individual with only a few thousands of investment dollars to the institution with many millions. I have endeavored to arrange the book in such a way that each will find it both simple to follow and helpful. Since one who has become steeped in the subject reaches rather quickly the point of thinking in mathematical terms, I found my primary problem to be one of keeping the explanations as simple and clear as possible, without sacrificing the more complicated possibilities which would interest the serious student. The following arrangement was therefore followed:

Part I contains a general explanation of investing formulas and the reasons why an increasing number of investors of all types are adopting them.

Part II is devoted to descriptions of the three basic methods for developing a formula plan to fit individual requirements and preferences. These have been arranged in the order of simplicity, progressing to the more complicated variations.

Part III consists of the working details of nine different formula plans which are currently in use by institutions or individuals. In some respects these go into greater detail than the descriptions in the preceding section. Some contain ideas for "refinements" such as forms of delaying actions which are omitted from Part II in the interest of simplicity. The reader's use of this section can depend entirely upon the extent of his interest.

Part IV is primarily intended for the investor who is still in the process of accumulating his investment fund. It is devoted to the subject of "dollar averaging" which, properly speaking, is not a formula plan in the ordinary sense of the word. It is included because it is a closely related subject and meets the broad definition of a successful method of investing which requires no forecast of stock market trends.

A tremendous amount of statistical work necessarily went into the preparation of this book. All data have been computed and checked as carefully as possible, but it is too much to hope that no inaccuracies have crept in. It is reasonable to assume, however, that no statistical error of sufficient magnitude to alter the basic conclusions is a major possibility.

LUCILE TOMLINSON

Port Washington, New York
September 15, 1947

# PART I

# GENERAL INFORMATION

CHART 1 DOW–JONES INDUSTRIAL AVERAGE 1915–1946

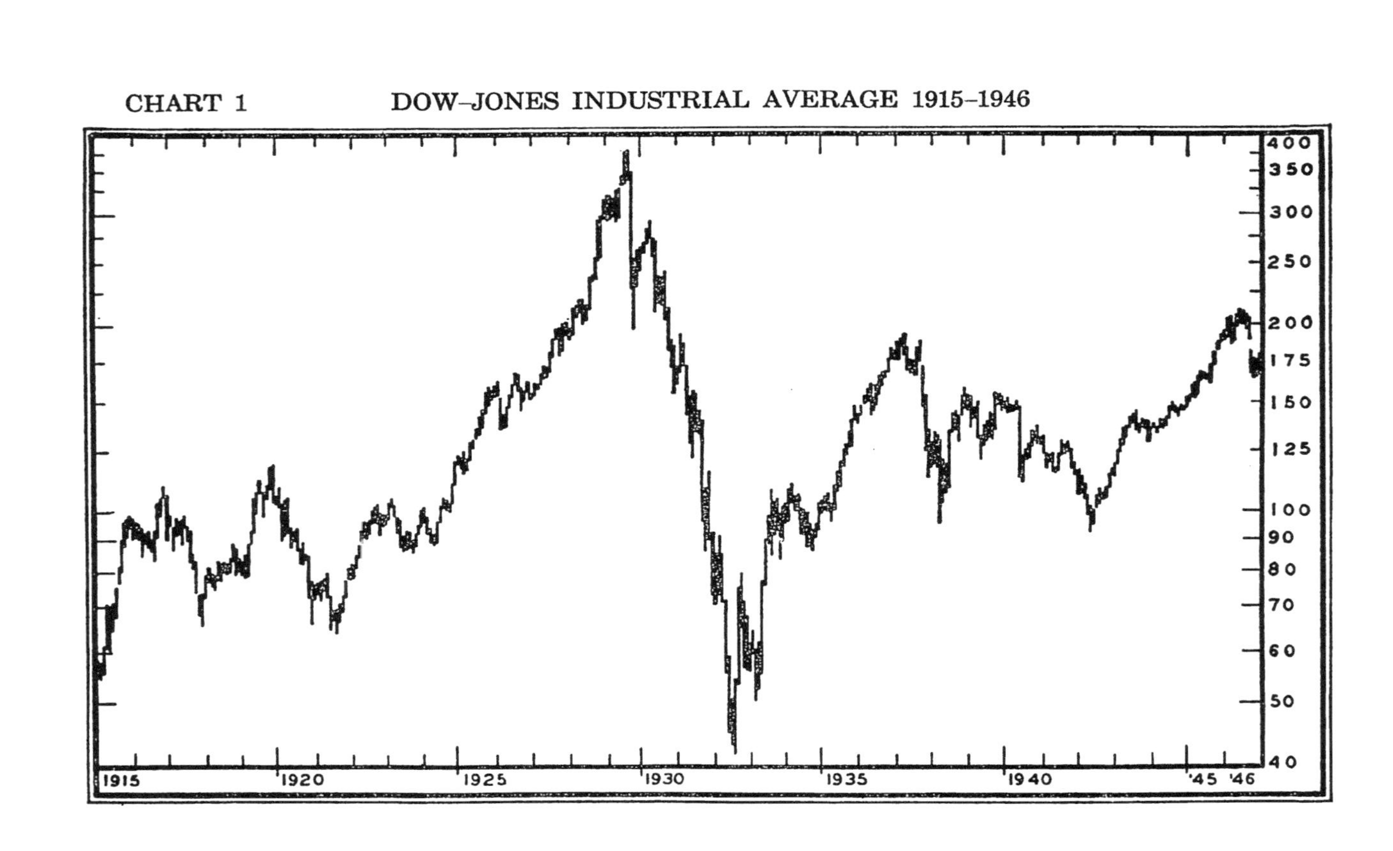

# CHAPTER I

## From "Buy and Hold" to Formula Planning

Soon after the stock market crash of late 1946, an investor who is by no means unsophisticated looked at the latest stock quotations in disgust and remarked ruefully, "Well, I've done it again. Held on right up to the top—and I'm still holding, just the way I did in 1929 and 1937.

"What makes me so mad at myself is I've learned it's time to get out of stocks when new issues start to go badly, the way they did last spring. But business was good and all the signs indicated it would get better; everybody was talking about inflation, and I was sure the industrial average would go to 250.

"The worst of it is, I can't buy anything now—when some issues look so cheap—because my capital is all tied up in the stocks I already own."

This investor put his finger on the precise reason why "investing formulas" or "formula plans" have been coming into widespread use in recent years. Not to be confused with methods or formulas for forecasting the market, they are simply a means of taking the emotional factor out of investing. Basically, they are methods designed to force an investor automatically to take at least part of his profits when prices are rising and to buy stocks when prices are lower. They do this by setting in advance the conditions under which money will be transferred from stocks to bonds, or vice versa.

An investing formula is first of all a means of preserving capital, of avoiding the losses which inevitably result from buying stocks when everybody is optimistic and prices are high, and selling them when the outlook is dim and prices are low. It is also a means of building up capital over the years, for a well-designed formula is bound to produce a certain amount of long-term gain and it is possible to achieve a degree of appreciation which should satisfy even the confirmed speculator.

The trend toward investing by formula is an outgrowth of several changes in investment thinking which have occurred in the past generation. For most investors, the 1929-1932 bear market brought to an abrupt end the belief that "sound" common stocks should be bought and held, i.e., thought of as long-term investments that would prove profitable in the end regardless of when they were bought. Investment "timing" became the goal of investors the world over. Statisticians and chartists had a field day during the decade of the 1930's and produced any number of remarkable devices which would have shown clearly in 1929 that it was time to get out of all common stocks. But unfortunately, few of these devices or "systems" indicated with equal clarity in the spring of 1937 that it was again time to get out of stocks; and if they did, the inflation psychology of the time convinced even the statisticians that the sale of stocks should be postponed.

And so once again the great majority of investors went into a bear market fully invested in common stocks, many of which fell to 25% or less of their previous prices. As investors picked themselves up from the ground in the summer of 1938, three things began to happen. There was a renewed, more strenuous search for better methods of forecasting price trends. Simultaneously, investors began seeking companies which, because of relative youth and interest in new products and ideas, might be expected to grow in the future, thus making their securities become more valuable. The term "growth stock" was added to the vocabulary of Wall Street and the stock of almost any company which had earned more in 1937 than it had in 1929 took on an aura of glamour. It was a return to the "common stocks for long-term investment" school of thought but with a far greater element of selectivity.

And finally, there was a small number of investors who said to themselves: Never again, and this time we mean it. We've learned that we'll never be able to take an objective viewpoint when everyone else is convinced the stock market is far from the top—or bottom—and prices are still rising rapidly, or falling. Since we can't bring ourselves to sell near the top or buy near the bottom, we'll have to find some other way to avoid losing part of our capital every time the stock market goes up and down.

These investors started to explore the possibilities of basing their procedure upon nothing more than a conviction that security prices would continue to go up and down. They found that there were a number of simple ways to derive moderate profits from market fluctuations without having to forecast either the direction or extent, and at the same time to assume less risk in stock investment than they had been taking in the past. Formula planning was born prior to 1938 but that is the year in which it first took a real lease on life.

All three investment approaches which developed after the 1938 decline or were accelerated by it still have their adherents. But when the smoke began to clear away from the debris left by the sudden market drop in the autumn of 1946, there were a good many investors who cast envious glances at the "formula planners" who were sitting calmly by, hoping that prices would go lower. For once again, emotional thinking had kept the great majority of investors from doing the right thing, even if a chart, index or just plain common sense had told them the time to start selling stocks had come.

Picking "growth stocks," too, had proved to be something less than simple. While a good number had behaved as expected, the price performance of such widely-acclaimed growth issues as Philip Morris and International Nickel was beginning to cast doubts upon the theory that growth stock investors could safely ignore market fluctuations.

Investors using formula plans had been selling stocks steadily as the rise progressed. Few were completely out of the market when the decline came, but they had substantial reserves of cash and high-grade bonds which they could re-invest at levels below those at which they had sold. Rather than bemoaning the decline, they were hoping it would continue for a time.

Much of the original work in the development of formula planning was done by institutional investors—colleges, insurance companies and trust companies. Proportionately, investing formulas are probably still in wider use among this type of investor than among individuals. But the formula method is just as adaptable to the problem of the individual as to that of the institution and in many cases the need is even greater. As the success of the institutions has become more widely known, an increasing number of individuals have followed their lead, and it is reasonable to expect that many more will do so as time goes on. There is practically no investment fund too small to use an investing formula, if the investor will take the time necessary to understand what he must do.

The purpose of this book is to explain the technique, the advantages and disadvantages of investing by formula. It is intended as a text-book. The author's philosophy, based upon fourteen years of close observation of the habits and accomplishments of both private and professional investors, might be summed up as follows:

A few individuals have over a long period of time demonstrated both sufficient investment "know-how" and control over their own emotions to do a better job without any formula plan than they could hope to achieve with one. This book is not for them. But these lucky ones have been rare.

The author is convinced the vast majority will find, if they will make a careful and honest computation of their past investment records, that they would be far better off if they had followed the simplest of investing formulas. This is the test which should determine in any individual case whether a formula plan should be adopted.

It is a test which, if at all possible, should be made. For of much greater importance than the specific details of any formula plan is the conviction with which it is adopted. You've got to stick to it to make it work. The whole purpose of a formula is to make you sell stocks when everybody seems to be buying them, and to buy stocks when everybody else is a deep shade of indigo. It won't seem right at the time and it may be a long while before you become glad you did it. That is why it is so very important both to be convinced at the start the whole thing is worth doing and to make the operation of the plan just as automatic as possible.

A formula plan is a substitute for management or judgment in only a limited sense. Once adopted, further judgment on the timing of aggregate stock purchases and sales is eliminated. But the plan does not remove the need for careful selection of the securities to be used and continuous supervision of those held, on a growth-stock basis or any other that seems desirable. And the choice of the plan itself calls for considerable judgment. There are several major types, capable of infinite variations, to fit the characteristics and objectives of a great variety of investors. Careful consideration must be given to many aspects and details so that temptation to change a plan *after* it has been adopted can be avoided.

Many examples are given in later chapters to indicate the range of results which hypothetical formula plans would have provided in the past, as well as several actual cases of plans which have been in operation for a number of years past. But the most valuable result, according to every investor who has employed the method, is one which cannot be measured.

Such an investor once put it this way: "You have no idea what a comfortable sensation it is to go to bed at night and know that I literally do not care whether the next movement in the Dow-Jones average is 100 points up or 100 points down. If it is up, I will take more profits. And if it is down, I will buy stocks back at a fraction of the prices at which I sold them."

How many investors are controlling their emotions by formula plans, or how many millions of investment dollars are managed in this way, can only be guessed. Considering the size of some of the institutional funds known to be guided by formula plans, as well as the extent to which the method has gained acceptance among individual investors, a sheer guess of a half a billion to a billion dollars in early 1947 is probably conservative.

It is interesting to contemplate the possible consequences if a much larger amount of stocks were in the hands of investors committed to selling as prices go up and buying as they go down. Assume for the moment that in another few years ten times the present amount of investment money were to be controlled by formula plans. The total value of all stocks listed on the New York Stock Exchange, preferred as well as common, has never been much above $80 billion.

Price swings as violent as many in the past twenty years would be impossible, for the formula planners would provide both a support in declines and a tempering influence on rises. True, the profits the formula planners themselves could expect would become considerably less. But with violent stock price fluctuations eliminated, investment hazards would be reduced all around.

Wall Street's emotional binges, some people claim, have a pernicious effect upon business sentiment. Instead of acting only as a barometer of business, the theory goes, the stock market has come to help determine the actual level of business. If this is true, widespread adoption of investing formulas would be of tremendous significance to the entire country.

# CHAPTER II

## Emotional Hazards

The psychological handicap under which most investors operate has probably never been more succinctly expressed than by Ray Morris, partner of Brown Brothers, Harriman & Company, in his explanation of Vassar College's adoption of a formula plan:

> "Ever since there have been security markets they have been affected by periodic waves of optimism and of pessimism. Without some sort of a plan which concentrates on the long view of the market, and more or less ignores what is happening currently, it seems to be human experience that trustees, like individuals, tend to buy stocks when they are doing well and to sell them when they are doing badly. But it requires a superhuman degree of alertness to operate a fund on that basis without shrinking it in the process."

Hopes, fears, wishful thinking and the inability to isolate one's own reasoning from that of "the crowd"—all help explain the regular cycle of investor emotion which is the strongest obstacle to success in the investing of money. When the trend has been down for some time, it is impossible to make a decision to buy stocks as long as prices continue to drop. Everyone else seems bearish at such a time and prices always look as if they were going a great deal lower. One inevitably hopes to buy "a little cheaper."

Eventually prices rise a bit. But now it becomes even more difficult to buy, because prices have already gone up and "there is bound to be a reaction." Finally, however, one decides that this time there isn't going to be any reaction and one had better buy before it is too late. The chances are frequently excellent that the market is close to a peak by the time this decision has been reached.

When the time comes to sell stocks, the same thing is likely to happen, in reverse. So long as prices are rising, the decision to liquidate part of one's stockholdings is even more difficult to make than buying them was in the first place. To sell stocks and then watch their prices continue rising is just about unbearable for most people, but selling *after* the decline is under way is not much easier and usually runs smack into the "I'll sell when they get back to their former highs" trend of thought. Normal procedure is to hold on, first in hope, then in despair, and finally decide the stocks were bought for income anyway, or else sell them out close to the low.

That this is no exaggeration of the typical investor's actions is borne out by such available statistics as volume of stock exchange transactions, the trend of odd-lot purchases and sales, and the public's purchases and redemptions of open-end investment company shares. And many professional investors and givers-of-investment-advice appear nearly equally subject to the same type of influences. Anyone who has spent much time following the daily market letters of brokerage houses, for example, can hardly be blamed for developing a distinctly skeptical attitude toward the market "predictions" which emanate from those who are closest to the buying and selling of securities. There is no question that a great deal of valuable research on individual securities is done by the statistical staffs of the large brokerage firms, but there is pitifully little evidence that a detached attitude toward the market can long be maintained by anyone in that atmosphere.

The point is not that stock market forecasting with a reasonable degree of accuracy is impossible; it is that an objective viewpoint and an ability to take independent action are so commonly impossible to achieve. Investors tend to be all bullish at once or all bearish at once, and the feeling that the majority must be right, no matter how often proved wrong, seems to be the hardest in the world to overcome.

This is at once the primary reason why some investors have decided to use a formula method of investing and the reason why the investor who uses a formula plan should train himself as far as possible to forget about the stock market, except when his plan calls for some action.

Under a formula plan, regardless of type, the investor decides *in advance* just what he is going to do if or when certain things happen. At any time, he will know what he is to do if the market goes up a certain amount and what he will do if the market goes down a certain amount. At the time he makes these decisions, he is presumably free from the emotions which are so certain to exist when the time comes for acting upon them. As part of his plan, he takes whatever steps he thinks will be necessary to enforce upon himself the action he has planned.

The difference between this and typical investor action can be illustrated by reference to the 1942-1946 bull market. When the industrial average first reached 150 in 1944 an investor remarked to the author that he thought the market was "good for 200" and that when it got there he'd be satisfied and sell out "every single share of stock" he owned. He made no sales along the way—in fact, added new money to his account whenever he could. By January 1946 the market had done all that he had expected of it and his unrealized profits were truly impressive.

But did he stick to the resolution he had made two years earlier? Unfortunately, he did not. Because "conditions had changed" in the meantime! Inflation, he declared, was going to take the industrial average easily up to 300 and he had raised his sights accordingly—at 300 he would sell "every single share of stock." History never proved the point, but it is logical to expect that if 300 had ever been reached, this investor would by then have been planning to sell out at 500.

For contrast, let us assume that another investor started to operate under a formula plan at the same time in 1944. He might have decided that after a 20% rise in the industrial average he would reduce his stock holdings by 20% and that after each subsequent 15% rise he would sell an additional 15% of his stocks. (He would have planned what he would do if the market went down, too, but since it didn't, that part of the plan will be ignored for the purpose of this example.) He would have put the plan into writing and told his broker or his investment dealer that he wanted this action taken even if he himself kicked to high heaven when the time came.

The time came. At 180 in 1945 20% of his stocks would have been sold and the proceeds put safely away in the bank or government bonds. He would probably have been quite unhappy as the market kept on going up and it would not be surprising if his broker or dealer had quite a tussle with him when the next sell level—206—was reached a few months later and his plan called for the further liquidation of 15% of his remaining stocks. But the plan and the steps he had taken when the plan was adopted would have kept his emotions from controlling his actions and the sale would have been made.

Unlike the first investor, he would have had money with which to buy stocks some time later on when prices were lower and yields higher than when the sales were made. And he probably would have become sufficiently convinced of the merits of adopting a formula and *sticking to it* that he would find it considerably easier the next time to obey the dictates of his plan.

# CHAPTER III

## OUTLINE OF FORMULA PLANNING

ALL FORMULA plans* have a good many characteristics in common. First and most important is the requirement that the investment fund consist of two main parts: one is usually made up of cash, bank deposits, or securities whose prices remain fairly stable, such as bonds of at least good grade, or high-grade preferred stocks; the other consists of securities whose prices move up and down, such as common stocks, speculative preferred stocks and defaulted bonds.

The first part is sometimes described as the "defensive" or "stable" portion of the fund, and the second part as the "aggressive" or "volatile" portion. For the sake of simplicity, the terms "bond" and "stock" are used in this book to describe the stable and volatile portions of the fund respectively, but the terms are intended to include the other types of securities mentioned.

It is perfectly possible to use a formula plan even if the entire fund is invested either in stocks or in bonds, provided that these include two grades of stocks or two grades of bonds. The working of any plan depends simply upon the existence of two types or classes of securities, one of which moves up and down faster than the other. But the effectiveness of the plan depends upon how much *difference* there is between the fluctuations of the two classes. The greater the difference, the better the long-term capital results will be.

For this reason, neither an all-bond nor an all-stock program is as ideal for formula plan purposes as a fund in which both are used. For the same reason, the maximum gain under a formula

*With the exception of Dollar Averaging, discussed in Part IV, which strictly speaking is not a formula plan.

plan will generally be in a fund which is made up of the highest-grade bonds (or cash) on the defensive side, and of the fastest-moving type of speculative stocks on the aggressive side.

The plan itself consists of arrangements for transferring funds from the stock side to the bond side, or vice-versa, under specific, pre-determined conditions. The amounts and intervals will vary according to the particular plan being used, but all have the effect of forcing the sale of some stocks in a prolonged period of rising prices and the purchase of some stocks when prices are falling.

The plan may simply require that a fixed *proportion* of the fund is to be kept in common stocks. (See Constant Stock-Bond Ratio, Chapter IX). In this case, relatively small sales or purchases will be made and the size of the stock fund will not change greatly from time to time. The investor will have approximately the same *percentage* of his fund in stocks at the top of a rise as he has at the bottom of a decline, but he will have fewer *shares* at the top than at the bottom.

Or the plan may require the *proportion* of stocks to be reduced as prices rise and increased as they fall. (See Variable Stock-Bond Ratio, Chapters X to XIV). Sales and purchases will be considerably larger under this type of plan, and stocks in the fund may, if the investor wishes, range all the way from 0% to 100%.

The formula plan investor is required to take a long-term view of what he is doing. Since he usually starts to sell stocks before the top of a rise is reached, there are bound to be times when, if he is measuring from the beginning of the rise, his fund will be worth less than if he had taken no action at all. Conversely, if he measures from the top down, he may find that after making some purchases he has suffered more depreciation than if he had sat tight with only what he held at the top.

The proper way to measure results is to take a period of time when the stock market, as measured by an index such as the Dow-Jones industrial average, went down and up, or up and down, but ended right where it started. Every formula plan virtually guarantees, provided stock prices have moved sufficiently to bring the plan into action (and the securities held have not deviated from the market), that the fund will be worth more at the end of such a period than at the beginning. Obviously, if it had been fully invested throughout the period, its value would be the same as at the beginning. If random purchases and sales of stocks had been made under the guidance of the investor's emotions it would in all probability be worth less than at the start.

It should be clear by now that true gains are derived from the use of a formula plan only as the result of stock market declines. The further down the market goes, the bigger the gains will eventually be—provided only that the investor sticks strictly to his plan and that the particular securities he holds do not simply go down and stay down. On the latter point, formula planning is based on the assumption that security prices in general will continue to move in both directions; to insure that the particular securities the investor holds do not go counter to the trend is a problem of selection which is discussed in a later chapter.

The assumption that securities in general will continue to fluctuate is not frequently questioned. However, the related question of whether they will necessarily continue to fluctuate in about the same general range as they have in the past is less easily answered. Presumably it is possible that the Dow-Jones industrials might rise, say, to 500 and then fluctuate between 300 and 500; or drop to 50 and then move only between 50 and 100.* Various means have been used in some formula plans to keep them in step with any basic change in the stock market, but the investor who considers either of such extreme occurrences a possibility should know that no formula plan will give him ideal protection against either a permanent inflation or permanent deflation in common stock prices. It just can't be done.

*The range since 1935 has been from about 100 to a little over 200 and the highest and lowest levels reached since 1910 were 381 in 1929 and 41 in 1932.

Another limitation common to most formula plans is the difficulty of devising any plan which will both obtain the maximum advantage from the broad swings of the market—such as that from 1942 to 1946—and at the same time be certain of deriving some advantage from the shorter or "intermediate" movements such as those in 1940 and 1941. Of the two possibilities, the potential gains from the long swings appear so much greater than those from the short ones that most plans choose the former alternative. But the investor should understand that patience is an important item of the formula planner's equipment. Depending upon the type of market he encounters after starting his plan, he may have to wait a considerable time for concrete evidence of its effectiveness.

Most investors still vividly recall the 1929-1932 stock market experience and consequently want to know how any formula plan they are considering would have worked during that period. (For those who don't remember the details: the industrial average climbed to a high of 381 in September, 1929, and subsequently fell to a low of 41 in July, 1932, before starting back up.) The period presents a problem to formula planners. So far as is known, no formal plan was in actual use at the time, so that any estimates of results must at best be based upon conjectures.

Some of the plans in this book would have worked reasonably well; others, because they would have called for purchases too early in the decline and sales too soon after the 1932 lows, would not. The best results would have been obtained from the Variable Ratio type plans. From Chart 2 on Page 18, which shows a 50-year record for a hypothetical Variable Ratio plan, a clear picture of performance during the period can be obtained.

Under any Variable Ratio plan devised now and worked back, however, the investor would have been almost completely out of stocks for about four years prior to the 1929 break, including the extreme period of "New Era" feeling. Many people find it hard to believe that any investor would have had sufficient strength of character at that time to withstand the terrific impact of popular sentiment—plan or no plan. It is more than likely that the investor who did continue using a plan would have set his sights much higher than hindsight proves advisable. He would nevertheless have kept more protection than he otherwise had, but his final result can only be guessed.

It is possible to devise automatic plans which would neatly fit a comparable situation in the future—for practical purposes, the Yale University plan can be described as of this type. Maximum advantage can be derived from a prolonged upswing and subsequent stock purchases postponed until something approaching 1931-1932 market conditions re-occurs. The trouble with doing so is that so much must be sacrificed in terms of potential profits from narrower movements.

Many formula planners prefer to follow a line of reasoning which goes something like this: Both the 1929 highs and the 1932 lows were completely abnormal. (As Chart 6 on page 88 shows, these were the only times in 50 years that the industrial average broke out of an otherwise clearly defined channel.) It is not likely that this particular bit of financial history will repeat itself, because economic and social conditions have changed so drastically in the meantime. With margin trading all but prohibited, as well as for other reasons, they do not believe there is a great possibility that stock prices in general will again break so far out of line on the upside; nor do they think that 1932 low levels will be seen again unless capitalism in the United States is completely doomed—and in that case, it won't make much difference what they do. Therefore, they largely exclude the entire 1927-1933 period from consideration in formula planning; they can provide a small degree of protection against its happening again, but they don't handicap themselves by considering it a probability.

### Frequency of Transactions

Another question often asked concerns the frequency and number of transactions called for under a formula plan. The

CHART 2 HYPOTHETICAL $1,000,000 FUND 1897–1946

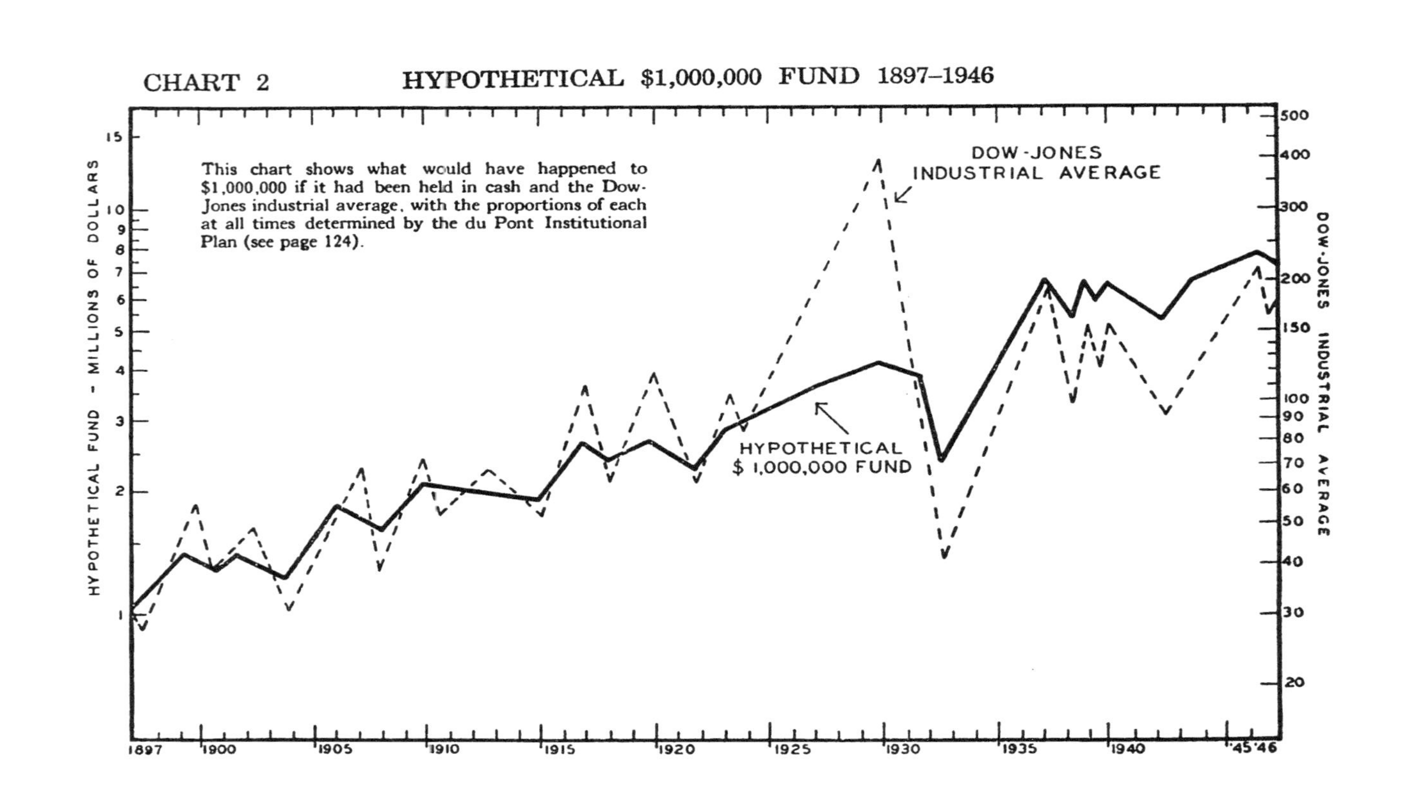

investor's preference in this respect, and also the size of his fund, should be considered in devising or selecting the plan. The frequency of worthwhile price advances and declines will determine the number of important changes in any event, but the conditions he sets for himself can be made to control how often action of some kind is taken.

In this connection, there is a good argument for requiring regular action at reasonably frequent intervals, such as every three or six months, whether or not a substantial transfer of capital is involved. The formation of good habits is as important in following a formula plan as it is in any other activity. Sooner or later the investor is going to come to a point at which his plan requires him to do something—whether it is to sell stocks while prices are rushing up or to buy them when prices seem headed for the hurricane cellar—which his entire nature will resist doing. There is a far better chance he will carry out the required action if he has formed the habit of automatically making some change at not too infrequent intervals.

There is the additional possibility that if a plan has required no action over a period of several years, it will have been forgotten entirely by the time a point requiring the purchase or sale of securities is reached. A good deal depends upon the individual, but for most, a plan that calls for at least an annual adjustment of the stock-bond ratio has an advantage not to be overlooked.

## Income

The effect of a formula plan upon current income is another logical question raised by many investors. There is no arbitrary answer that can be given—it depends upon the plan, the types of securities used, and how the money would otherwise have been invested. Eventually, if the plan produces the increase in capital reasonably to be expected, income is likely to be higher, regardless of these considerations, for the simple reason that the earning assets of the fund have been increased. But since it may take some years to achieve this happy condition, the immediate effect must also be considered.

If a fund previously invested in high-yielding stocks and bonds is converted into highest-grade bonds, on the one hand, and extremely speculative common stocks (and therefore probably low-income producers), on the other, there is bound to be an immediate decline in income. Only the investor concentrating upon capital growth would want to—or would be in a position to—go that far.

If it is assumed that approximately the same division between stocks and bonds would have been made without the formula plan and the same types of issues bought, then an increase in income under the plan is a good possibility almost right from the start. (This assumes that the stocks held yield more than the bonds.) For the plan forces additional purchases of stocks when prices are lower and yields generally higher.

Aside from these generalizations, the best answer to the question of income is probably the fact that the longest-standing users of formula plans are institutional investors, such as colleges, whose primary investment objective is income.

## Taxes

The penalty in the United States for making profits in securities is the payment of capital gains taxes (except when the investor is a non-taxable institution.) The formula planner may find himself paying heavier taxes than he would without a plan, but only because he has realized more profits. The only certain way to avoid paying capital gains taxes is the obvious one of never having or taking profits.

Under a formula plan, it is a simple matter to arrange that only *long-term* profits are ever taken—i.e., profits on securities held over six months, the effective tax on which is only half the investor's regular rate or a maximum of 25%. It seldom happens that sales are required less than six months after a purchase, and when it does, the investor, unless he has just started his program, is certain under most types of plans to have other shares which were bought at an earlier date.

Aside from handling specific stock certificates in order to minimize capital gains taxes, it is contrary to the basic purpose of formula planning to let tax considerations interfere with the automatic working of any plan. The formula planner believes it is better to keep some of his profits—minus taxes—than to let them disappear.

### Additions to the Fund

It is common experience that new money for investment is usually available at the worst time to invest it. Incomes are higher when security prices are high; donors are more generous to institutional and charitable funds.

The question of how to invest new money is easily answered under any formula plan. Whatever stock-bond ratio is then controlling is automatically applied to the additional money, under most plans. This procedure alone is reported by investors to have justified their use of a formula, without regard to the effect of the plan on previously-existing funds.

Many investors are in a position where current additions to their investment fund are relatively more important than their accumulated capital. Their problem is somewhat different from that of the investor who has already accumulated the major portion of his wealth. Their attention is directed to the final section of this book, on the subject of "Dollar Averaging," a unique type of planning particularly appropriate to their situation.

# CHAPTER IV

## Institutional Investors

A cynic has said that any time five investment men unanimously agree it is time to buy common stocks, it is probably a good time to sell them. Anyone who has worked with an institutional investment committee would retort by asking whether it is ever possible at all to get five investors to agree on such a point.

Whatever the case, it is a fact that institutions such as colleges, insurance companies, and trust companies, which operate under the supervision of a Finance Committee, have a compelling additional reason for their interest in formula plans: they are a means of getting action from a group. So far as is known, every institution which has operated under a plan agrees on the basic point that use of a formula has expedited the work of its Finance Committee, enabled the Committee to concentrate on the best possible selection of individual securities, and has produced better results than were the previous experience.

From Vassar comes the report that in eight and one-half years of operation under the common stock control plan there has not been a disagreement among Finance Committee members in regard to the purchase or sale of stocks. From Oberlin College, where the experience is of a shorter duration and still somewhat in the experimental stage, comes the statement: "The committee used to spend two-thirds of its time debating whether stocks should be increased or decreased and one-third deciding on individual issues. Now the proportions are reversed."

It is also customary in many cases for the composition of a Finance Committee to change in part every year or two. A formula plan, according to Yale University, provides a continuous form of positive control and enables the Committee at any time to know exactly where the fund stands and what has gone before.

There are other advantages of particular significance for institutional-type investors. Since a plan can be set up so as to work automatically, it can take care of protracted periods between committee meetings. If, for example, there is a sudden sharp drop in security prices (such as the May 1940 experience), purchases can be made without waiting for a regular meeting date or calling a special one.

A trust company can set up plans for individual accounts in such a way as to reduce considerably the amount of time and effort required for proper supervision. This would appear to be of particular significance in the case of smaller trust funds.

Despite these special advantages, institutional investors all appear to agree that the biggest benefits lie in the emotional control a plan provides. A plan is "a stabilizing factor in mental approach to portfolio management," according to the treasurer of Massachusetts Institute of Technology, which has operated under an informal type of plan since 1932. "It protects a finance committee against its own emotions," according to another experienced planner.

Most of the plans cited as examples in this book are "institutional" plans. Even institutions with presumably much the same investment objectives and problems—such as two comparable colleges—have adopted different types of formula plans. This illustrates the fact that a formula plan should fit not only the circumstances but also the temperaments and preferences of the individual investor. Finance committees are made up of individuals, and experience has proved that an institutional plan works most efficiently when every committee member is personally convinced the arrangement is a good one.

Some of the institutions quoted have set up inflexible rules and followed them precisely when the time for action came. Others either have less formal plans or simply give themselves a certain amount of leeway in following the dictates of the plan. Some institutions, for example, began to purchase stocks around the low levels of 1946, even though a strict interpretation of their plans would have postponed all purchases to a lower level.

Since a great deal of emphasis has been given in an earlier chapter to the importance of obeying implicitly the requirements of a plan, once adopted, the attitude of the institutions which have taken a contrary position warrants discussion. The evidence available as to the relative merits of flexibility and inflexibility in following a formula plan is admittedly inconclusive, but certain tentative conclusions can perhaps be drawn from an examination of statements based on experience.

One manager of a large fund which has operated under a plan for more than five years declared that a formula should be considered the background against which a position is tested. "It makes you face up to your position at times when your emotions are leading you in the opposite direction." Said another, "If you don't sell stocks when your plan says you should, you at least take a mighty careful look at every single stock in your portfolio and make very sure you can justify its retention. You automatically scale up the quality even if you don't scale down the total."

In justification of purchases that were made in 1946 before the plan called for them, a college investment officer pointed out that the plan had been followed quite rigidly on the way up and as a result his institution had a fair amount of cash obtained from sales of stocks at much higher prices than then existed. The Committee felt there was a reasonable doubt under conditions then existing whether their purchase level would be reached before stock prices again turned up and that some protection against that possibility was warranted. So long as sufficient buying power was preserved to take advantage of lower prices, if they did develop, and *no purchases were made above the levels of the corresponding sales*, he felt that discretion, in this case, was the better part of formula planning.

The other side of the picture is the occasional institution which was willing, late in 1946, to admit that it wished its plan had been followed more rigidly during the previous year or two, when sales were called for but not made, or not made completely. They felt their Committees would hesitate in the future to take any action contrary to their plans.

It might be pointed out here that a committee-directed institutional fund is in a somewhat different position from the ordinary individual investor when it comes to deciding how much discretion should be allowed under a formula plan. On average, the institutional fund may be holding more conservative securities and following a more conservatively-designed plan, under which current income considerations have been given greater weight than appreciation possibilities. If so, it may have less to lose by failure to follow a plan strictly.

Probably more important, an institution is under greater compulsion to keep its plan in mind, whether or not it is followed strictly. The individual who decides once he "won't bother this time" and from there on forgets about the whole thing has only his own conscience to bother him if his judgment later on is proved faulty. The committee members who have officially adopted a plan have to answer first to each other and second to their "bosses," whether they be stockholders, trust beneficiaries, or alumni.

Advisers who have had experience with individual investors in the use of formula plans state almost without qualification that the investor who is going to adopt a formula plan must make up his mind to stick to it through thick and thin and do what it tells him to do, *when* it tells him to do it. The one possible exception, which can only be made after a plan has been in operation for some time, is taking action *before* it is called for. In buying stocks, care must be taken that no more money is used than was taken out of stocks at a higher level; in selling them, that no more are sold than were bought at lower levels. The procedure is not necessarily recommended, but it is the one way in which judgment can be mixed with formula planning without danger of actual loss, and there are a few times under any formula plan when it would have proved profitable.

# CHAPTER V

## SELECTION OF SECURITIES

A FORMULA plan is a solution for only one part of the investment problem; namely, the timing of increases and decreases in the total amount of common stocks held. It has nothing to do with the problem of selecting the individual securities which make up an investor's portfolio.

Under a formula plan, there is still every reason for making the best possible choice of specific stocks and bonds to be held, and changes from one particular issue to another in the same classification are made just as if no plan were being followed.

The only difference in regard to security selection with and without a formula plan is that the "best possible choice" is not necessarily the same under the two methods. It may or may not be, depending upon the investor's particular objective.

If capital protection and immediate income are the sole or principal objectives, the investor will presumably concentrate on selecting individual issues in the strongest positions with the best prospects for future enhancement of value. He can, if he likes, combine a "growth stock" policy with a formula plan and figure that he has a form of double protection against whatever the future may bring.

Diversification is, of course, just as desirable as if he were not using a plan. If the fund is a large one, this will not present an important problem; the investor can presumably also obtain competent assistance, if necessary, in the selection and supervision of his holdings. If his fund is comparatively small—say, less than the $100,000 minimum most investment counsellors require—he can obtain both diversification and supervision, as well as many additional conveniences, through the use of investment company shares, which are described more fully later in this chapter.

In an account in which capital growth is the primary objective, and future income more important than immediate, the choice of securities involves certain other considerations. For best capital results, investing under a formula plan requires that the stocks used not only be reasonably certain to keep up with the stock market in general but also have as high a degree of volatility as is consistent with the income and safety requirements of the investor.

The ideal type of stock for use with a formula plan is one which combines long-term growth possibilities with a high degree of volatility. In other words, the ideal is the type of stock which consistently goes up faster than the market average and declines more slowly. There are not many well-known issues, however, which offer hope of meeting this requirement. Most often, the investor seeking maximum capital appreciation must choose between the type of stock which has good growth prospects but only moderate volatility, and the type which can be expected to move up and down rapidly but has limited long-term growth characteristics.

A simple hypothetical example illustrates the difference in effect between volatility alone and growth characteristics with lower volatility. Assume that the market average starts at 150, declines to 100, and advances again to 150. The plan, we will say, calls for a 50% stock position at 150 and an 80% stock position at 100. The prices of a volatile stock and a slower-moving growth stock might compare as follows at these levels:

| Market Average | Volatile Stock | Growth Stock |
|---|---|---|
| 150 | 20 | 20 |
| 100 | 5 | 15 |
| 150 | 20 | 30 |

If a $20,000 fund were involved in both cases, the values when the market index returned to 150 would be:

| | |
|---|---|
| Fund using volatile stock | $42,500 |
| Fund using growth stock | 31,500 |

The reasons for the difference are that when additional money was added to the stock fund, at 100, so many more shares of the volatile stock than of the growth stock would be purchased, and the fact that the volatile stock then rose percentagewise further than the growth stock.

As a general rule, volatile securities present less difficulty in selection, and are more certain to perform as desired, than growth stocks. But the use of volatile securities requires even broader diversification than the use of investment-grade stocks, and the requirements of careful selection and continuous supervision are just as important. The first problem is to select issues which are likely to move consistently faster than the market—but only as much faster as is desired, since declines as well as rises are contemplated. Most securities have determinable "habits" in this respect; over the years they normally move at about the same rate in relation to a general index—more slowly, about the same, faster, or a great deal faster—in both rises and declines. Study of a great many statistics is necessary to determine which is which, and to catch the issues whose characteristics may change over the years.

Broad diversification is essential for several reasons. In the first place, there is no way to be certain that any individual issue will continue to behave in the future as it has in the past, whether it is a "blue chip" or the rankest speculation. The average of a large group of similar issues, on the other hand, is more likely to continue acting in "typical" fashion. Low-priced common stocks as a class, for example, have always moved up and down faster than the usual market indexes and will doubtless continue to do so, even though some individual low-priced issues never go far in either direction.

Of equal or greater importance is the reduction of risk which diversification provides. The greater the volatility, the more important is this aspect. Stocks which go up and down rapidly usually do so because they represent companies in the "feast or famine" industries or are junior issues in complicated capital structures. In either case, the danger of financial difficulties which might bring about collapse of the company is likely to be present, and it is therefore essential to hold a broad list of different issues.

To sum it all up, security selection is no less a problem under a formula plan than without one, and if the better appreciation possibilities in using volatile securities are desired, it may easily be greater. For the wealthy institution or other large investor, this may not represent much of a problem. But most individuals are in a different situation. For them, formula planning by itself may be at best only a half-way measure.

### Investment Company Shares

There is a very logical answer to the problem of security selection, and that is the financial institution known as the investment company. A full discussion of the subject of investment companies would require a book in itself. However, it is impossible to ignore the close connection between investment company shares and formula planning. They not only solve the diversification-selection-supervision problem of the relatively small investor, but their conveniences have also attracted many large investors to their use in formula planning.

An investment company (or "investment trust") is a business organization whose single activity is the investment of other people's money. It is set up very much like any other type of corporation and its shares of stock represent a proportionate ownership of all the corporation's assets. But instead of using the money paid in by shareholders to buy plant and equipment, for example, to start a manufacturing business, the investment company goes out and buys securities, just as an individual might. Its assets are then the actual securities, its income is the dividends and interest it receives on them, and its business consists of selecting and supervising the list of securities, known as the company's portfolio. The earnings of the business are paid out in the form of dividends to the shareholders.

The investment company, of course, has many shareholders, and its total assets are usually worth many millions of dollars. This enables the investment company to buy a great many different securities, thereby obtaining broad diversification, and to hire well-trained people to spend their entire working time doing the job of supervising. The cost of the supervision and other running expenses of the investment company are divided among all the shareholders, in proportion to the number of shares they hold, so that it is relatively low for all.

Each share of investment company stock, therefore, actually represents the ownership of fractional shares of a great many individual well-known securities. This way, $100 can obtain just as much diversification as $100,000—and exactly the same supervision. The price of the investment company stock goes up and down with the average value of the securities the investment company holds.

The majority of investment companies are known as "open-end" companies, or "mutual funds." These companies are continuously willing to redeem their shares or to issue new ones, so that the investor never has a problem in finding a buyer or a seller, and he can usually know before he buys or sells his shares just what the price is going to be. For these reasons particularly, this type of investment company is the most convenient for use with a formula plan.

In addition, several open-end investment companies have set up series of specialized separate funds, all under the same management but each one holding a different type of security, such as different grades of bonds or preferred stocks, "blue chip" common stocks, low-priced common stocks, etc., or the securities of separate industries. These funds are kept as close to fully invested as possible at all times, which is what the formula planner desires. Among these "specialized" funds are many which are particularly useful in applying a formula plan. The bond funds, for example, simplify both the problem of selection and—of perhaps greater importance to the small investor—the problem of purchases or sales in amounts of less than $1,000. Bonds are usually issued in $1,000 denominations, whereas shares of bond *funds* may be bought or sold in amounts of $100 or even less.

In the common stock department, the investor can choose almost precisely the degree of volatility he wants in that portion of his fund. To illustrate, Table 1 shows how nine representative specialized common stock funds performed during the stock market advances and declines between May 1940 and May 1947.

TABLE 1

PRICE CHANGES OF INVESTMENT COMPANY SHARES

PERCENTAGE CHANGES IN TWO RISES AND TWO DECLINES OF TYPICAL SPECIALIZED OPEN-END FUNDS*

| | 1940 Low to Nov. 1940 High | Nov. 1940 High to 1941-2 Low | 1941-2 Low to 1946 High | 1946 High to May 1947 Low |
|---|---|---|---|---|
| Dow-Jones Ind. Avge. | +24% | −33% | +129% | −23% |
| *Funds Holding Investment-type Common Stocks* | | | | |
| Company A | +25% | −32% | +113% | −26% |
| Company B | +24% | −29% | +153% | −30% |
| Company C | +34% | −32% | +124% | −34% |
| *Funds Holding Moderately Volatile Common Stocks* | | | | |
| Company D | +50% | −32% | +178% | −43% |
| Company E | # | −33% | +228% | −41% |
| Company F | +45% | −35% | +251% | −41% |
| *Funds Holding Speculative Common Stocks* | | | | |
| Company G | +42% | −41% | +678% | −48% |
| Company H | +52% | −42% | +327% | −49% |
| Company J | # | −42% | +355% | −53% |

*Percentage changes are based upon prices of specific existing funds; they are adjusted for dividends paid from realized profits but do not include ordinary dividends.

#Company not in existence in early 1940.

The convenience aspect of investment company shares is an important one. They virtually eliminate the problem of *what* to buy or sell when the time comes, since in buying or selling investment company shares the investor is automatically increasing or decreasing proportionately every one of the securities in the company's portfolio. His bookkeeping and safe-keeping problem is simplified since a single stock certificate and a single dividend check may represent a wide list of holdings.

Open-end investment company shares are always available when required and can always be liquidated in any quantity without any concession in price—unlike many individual securities where a single large order for either purchase or sale may force the price up or down in the process of execution.

Furthermore, the "stability" of the quoted price of open-end investment company shares enables the formula planner to know exactly what he is doing and what it will cost him. The prices, usually computed twice a day, normally remain in effect for several hours or over-night. The investor can find out the price at which a purchase (and in some cases a sale) can be made, take time to compute the number of shares necessary to fulfill the condition of his plan, and be certain that he will get exactly that price. There is no other type of security of which this is equally true.

Open-end investment company shares are sold by investment dealers throughout the country. The price of the shares includes a selling charge or commission which in one lump figure takes the place of all of the costs, direct and indirect, which the investor who buys other types of securities must pay. These include brokerage commissions, odd-lot fees and taxes, which are the direct costs, and the difference between what must be paid for a stock and what can be obtained for it at the same time (usually the "spread" between the bid and asked quotations), which is an indirect cost.

Many investment companies, instead of specializing in any particular type of security, do a general job of investment management. They may at times hold a considerable portion of their assets in cash or bonds, and at other times be fully invested in common stocks. Their selection of particular issues is guided by research departments at all times seeking the best available values in all fields of securities. These are known as "general management" companies and some of them have in the past produced excellent long-term results for their shareholders. (There are a few of these among what are known as "closed-end" investment companies which may also be suitable for use with a formula plan.)

This type of investment company might be considered comparable to a growth stock. If the management does a good job, the value will be higher after the market has completed a "round trip" than it was at the start. The question whether this type of company or one which concentrates primarily upon providing diversified volatility is more suitable for use with a formula plan is similar to the volatility vs. growth question already discussed.

In the examples of plans included in Part II, some additional light on the question is given by showing the hypothetical results for a period in the past of using classes of securities with various volatility characteristics and also of using a completely managed common stock fund. The investment company used to illustrate the latter point was intentionally selected because it had one of the best management records in the business for the period under consideration. In this respect, hindsight was used—it cannot be assumed that an investor would be equally fortunate in his choice.

All of the examples point to the same conclusion: In the long run, greater capital appreciation under a formula plan is obtained by using fast-moving classes of securities than by using growth issues with average volatility. However, the examples also show that temporary depreciation, when a decline occurred before any profits could be stored up, was greater when highly volatile securities were used.

Whether he is using investment company shares or individual securities, the investor needs to weigh the relative importance of growth of capital and growth of income, on the one hand, and utmost capital safety at all times and immediate income, on the other.

This explanation of investment companies is necessarily brief and cannot, of course, give details for the many individual companies now in existence. The interested reader is referred to the excellent and very complete reference book, published annually by Arthur Wiesenberger & Company of 61 Broadway, New York City, under the title, "Investment Companies." This book, in the preparation of which the author has served as Editorial Consultant for a number of years, includes pertinent statistical data on every company of any important size, as well as a tremendous amount of general information.

# CHAPTER VI

## Arithmetic Primer

Details of formula planning make desirable a familiarity with certain very simple mathematical processes. The more seriously the investor is interested in understanding *why* a plan works and in making his own computations, the greater is his need for statistical background. However, it is also perfectly possible to use a formula plan without much, or even any, knowledge of mathematics. Under the simplest plan of all, the investor is required to do nothing except compute at infrequent intervals the total market value of his securities.

Anyone who has completed the sixth grade of elementary school should have no difficulty in making the simple calculations necessary under *any* type of formula plan. For those whose memories are short and who consequently find percentage calculations somewhat baffling, the following brief "refresher course" is included:

1. *How to compute a percentage*

Under most formula plans, it is necessary at times to know what proportion of the total fund is represented by stocks and by bonds. This is a simple problem in division.

The total value, at market, of the holdings in each classification is first computed. The total of stocks, or the total of bonds, is then divided by the combined total, thus:

$$\frac{\text{Value of Stocks}}{\text{Total Value of Fund}} = \text{Percentage of Stocks to Total}$$

If the total fund is worth $50,000 and stocks are worth $20,000, the percentage of stocks is $20,000 divided by $50,000, which is .40, or 40%. The percentage of bonds is obviously the difference between 100% and this figure, or 60%.

2. *How to compute a percentage change in a price or market average*

This is also a simple problem in division followed by subtraction. The important thing to remember is that whether the price has gone up or down, the most recent price is always divided by the earlier one. If the price has gone from 100 to 125, divide 125 by 100, which gives 1.25. If the price has declined from 125 to 100, divide 100 by 125, which gives .80.

In both cases, the answers are in terms of 100%, so that subtraction is necessary. If the figure is less than 1, it is subtracted from 1 to get the percentage decline; e.g., 1 minus .80 equals .20, or a 20% decline.

If the figure is more than 1, subtract 1 from it to obtain the percentage gain; e.g., 1.25 minus 1 equals .25 or a 25% gain.

The process is just reversed if the problem is to find out what price level would be a certain percentage higher or lower than some other level. The desired percentage gain or decline must be expressed as a relative of 1 (as 1.25 for a 25% gain and .80 for a 20% decline) and this figure multiplied times the price. Thus, a 25% gain from 100 would be 1.25 times 100, or 125, while a 20% decline would be .80 times 100, or 80.

The slide rule is a very handy device for making all calculations of this type and the eventual saving in time should be well worth the slight effort of learning to use it.

3. *Equal percentage changes vs. equal numbers of points*

Formula plans are, or should be, built around percentage changes, rather than changes in number of points. A plan, for instance, may call for decreases in stock holdings at each successive 15% rise in the industrial average. This is slightly more complicated to compute than would be a plan which called for decreasing stocks at each 15-point rise, but there is a logical reason for preferring the former method.

From the 100 level, as an example, a 15% rise and a 15 point rise are identical. In either case, a $10,000 starting investment would have increased in value to $11,500. But from the 200 level, a 15 point rise would amount to only 7½%, or an increase in a $10,000 starting investment to $10,750.

When increases or decreases are expressed as percentages, the profits or losses are the same, regardless of the level of the market or the prices of the stocks held. This is both the reason for using percentages in formula plans, and the reason why the charts in this book are drawn on what are called logarithmic scales. All this means is that equal percentage changes occupy the same amount of space, so that one rise which would have doubled an investor's money looks like any other rise that would have done the same thing, even if one started from a price of 25 and the other from 125.

4. *Percentage gains and percentage losses*

When a percent *gain* is figured, the *smaller* figure is the divisor; when a percent *loss* is computed, the *larger* figure is the divisor. The result is that a 25% gain is really smaller than a 25% loss which follows that gain. If you buy a stock at 100, for example, and it goes up 25%, it is then worth 125. But now if it goes down 25%, it is worth only 75%, of 125, not quite 94.

Another way to visualize this important distinction is to realize that the largest possible loss is 100%, while profits have no upper limit. If a stock goes from 50 to 100, the gain is 100%. But if the stock turns around and goes from 100 back down to 50, the loss is not 100%, but only 50%.

For every percentage gain, there is a percentage loss which is equivalent in importance, or, to say the same thing a little differently, corresponds to the gain in number of points or dollar value. A 20% loss corresponds to a 25% gain—if a stock goes up 25% and then down 20%, it will be right back where it started. Mathematicians can easily figure out the basis for the relationships; others may find the following table of corresponding rises and declines of help in formula planning:

| Advance | Corresponding decline |
|---|---|
| 10% | 9.1% |
| 15 | 13.0 |
| 20 | 16.7 |
| 25 | 20.0 |
| 33.3 | 25.0 |
| 50 | 33.3 |
| 100 | 50.0 |

In formula planning, it is generally desirable to use the same levels on the way up as on the way down. To bring them out this way, it is necessary to use one percentage figure for calculating points *above* the starting level, and the corresponding decline percentage to compute those *below* the starting level.

5. *Market change required to produce specific change in stock-bond ratio*

A certain type of formula plan may call for an initial division between stocks and bonds of 50-50, with the provision that a change will be made when stocks rise sufficiently to make the ratio 55-45. (This is not the most common form of plan, but some investors have preferred it.)

Calculating the percentage rise in stock prices which would bring about such a change in the ratio is more complicated than it may appear. The best way to figure it is to remember that the value of the bond portion will be the same before and after. So if the original ratio is 50-50 and it is desired to find out what increase in common stocks will produce a 55-45 ratio, the total value of the fund after the rise will be the figure of which 45% equals the bond fund.

If the bond fund is $10,000, for example, then the problem is "$10,000 is 45% of what?" The answer is $10,000 divided by 45 and multiplied by 100, or $22,200. The stock portion, which also started at $10,000, would have to increase to $12,200, or by 22%, which is the desired figure.

The same formula can be used with any set of figures.

# PART II

# BASIC FORMULA PLANS

# CHAPTER VII

## How the Formulas Were Tested

For each basic type of plan, and for many of the possible variations, results are given in succeeding chapters for a series of hypothetical funds "managed" in accordance with the plan over a period in the past. The following points pertain to all of the tests:

1. *The 1937–1946 testing period*

On December 31, 1936, the Dow-Jones industrial average closed at 179.90; exactly ten years later it closed at 177.20. In between it had been as high as 212.50 and as low as 92.92, and if only the important movements are considered, the total ground it had covered amounted to about 400 points. For testing an automatic investment plan, the period is close to ideal. The investor who bought stocks at the beginning of the period and neither bought nor sold a share of stock during the ten years, would have had a very slight loss (about $1\frac{1}{2}\%$) at the end of the period, if his stocks moved just as the average did. To simplify it even further, it was assumed in the tests that the industrial average stood at exactly 180 at both ends of the ten-year period, so that the "buy-and-hold" investor can be considered to have come out exactly even.

The period is a comparatively recent one and it is hoped that the reader will be able to recall what his actual investment experience was during the time. This, as previously mentioned, is the really significant comparison to be made with the results of the hypothetical funds.

Ideally, the test of a formula plan should cover "all kinds of markets." With available statistical data, however, this is difficult. As much general comment as possible is given to the probable performance of the various plans under conceivable circumstances, and a few plans have been computed for the entire 1897–1946 period. These, presented in chart form, enable the reader to study the results in any type of market which occurred during those 50 years.

2. *The Dow-Jones Industrial Average*

For the common stock portion of the hypothetical funds, the Dow-Jones industrial average was used in all the basic tests. The choice was dictated by the availability of daily figures for the past 50 years and the fact that it is the best known of stock market indexes. It is a simple average of the prices of 30 well-known industrial stocks, computed hourly by Dow-Jones & Company, publishers of The Wall Street Journal, and published daily in many newspapers throughout the country. The complete record back to 1897 is contained in "The Dow-Jones Averages,"* which can be purchased from the publisher of this book.

While the industrial average is used to indicate the result of simply "buying and holding" common stocks, this is not strictly correct. Changes are made by Dow-Jones & Company in the stocks comprising the average from time to time in order to keep it representative of market action. Especially in the years prior to 1933, substitutions were made fairly frequently, and there is consequently little resemblance between the average of 1897 and that of 1947. The industrial average, in short, is used to represent the aggregate action of market leaders, but a certain amount of "management" is required to make any list of stocks comply with this condition over a period of years.

3. *The Volatility Indexes*

In following any type of formula plan, the best long-term capital results are obtained when the most volatile (i.e., fastest

*"The Dow-Jones Averages" Barron's Book Dept., Boston, Mass. Price $10.

moving) securities are used for the stock portion. To show the effects of differing degrees of volatility, indexes of specific classes of securities were used for some of the tests in the same manner as was the industrial average, which represents a diversified list of predominantly investment-type common stocks.

Three types of stocks are used as illustrations, designated as (1) "Business Cycle," (2) "Low-Priced" and (3) "Highly Speculative." The groups represent respectively:

(1) the leaders among well-established companies whose earnings fluctuate considerably over a business cycle;

(2) the more marginal type of company, usually having an erratic earnings record; and

(3) a diversified group of "leverage" investment company stocks—issues which, because of their companies' capital structures, are similar in many ways to margin accounts.

All three classes move faster than the industrial average, both up and down. The relationship between them may vary at different stages of a market cycle, but over broad swings the Business Cycle stocks tend to move about 1½ times the average, the Low-Priced stocks about twice, and the Highly Speculative issues about three times.

These three indexes, like the industrial average, are fully-invested positions in the designated classes of securities. While a certain amount of "management" is required to keep any index continuously representative of its type of security, there is no "timing" involved, either in selection of securities or in the handling of a cash position. To make the comparison as informative as possible, minor adjustments have been made in the indexes, where necessary, in order to make the 1946 closing level identical with that at the start of 1937. In other words, there would have been neither profit nor loss if any of the indexes had simply been "bought and held" for the entire ten years.

4. *The "Management" Index*

When the investor comes to the actual selection of securities to use in following a formula plan, he will probably want to consider the comparative advantages of using securities chosen for volatility characteristics alone and those which have "growth" possibilities—that is, offer the possibility that when a market cycle has been completed, they will be selling at levels higher than at the start. Among these might be included the individual stocks of companies in relatively new and growing businesses, and the shares of well-managed investment companies with diversified portfolios.

To show the hypothetical results of using this type of security under a formula plan, a fifth "index" is included. Designated as a "Fully-managed Stock Fund," it is based upon the share asset value of a diversified open-end investment company which had an outstanding performance record during the 1937–1946 period. After making the necessary adjustments for capital gains dividends paid out, the shares of this fund showed a "growth" of about 32% at the end of the period. Holdings of the fund consisted solely of common stocks or other equity-type securities and of cash and/or government bonds when a defensive position was desired. The average volatility shown by the price movements was somewhat greater than that of the industrial average.

In all tables, results are shown both for a plan using the fully-managed stock fund and for a straight, undisturbed investment in it. It is thus possible to compare the hypothetical formula plan results in various classes of securities with one of the best actual management records publicly available for the 1937–1946 period.

5. *Fractional Shares*

To simplify the calculations—and make them comparable with each other—no attempt was made in the tests to be realistic about the practical problem of investing a precise amount of money in units of stock. All tests are based on dollar amounts of stocks and bonds, rather than shares. The method therefore implies that fractional shares of stocks would have been bought when necessary—an obvious impossibility. The effect on the results, however, is insignificant. Spot checks indicate that it makes little or no difference in the end as long as the largest possible full number of shares is bought or sold when a change is required.

### 6. *The Bond Portion*

As previously explained, the "bond" portion of a formula plan account may, in actual practice, include bonds of various types, high-grade preferred stocks, savings accounts or cash. For testing purposes, it has been treated as if it were simply a fund of cash, with no fluctuations in market value. The chief virtue of this method is its simplicity for the calculator, but in practice the same effect can be achieved by carrying this side of the account at par value or book cost, disregarding minor fluctuations.

### 7. *Expenses*

No accurate computation of the costs of buying and selling securities under a hypothetical test is possible, unless it is assumed that open-end investment company shares are the medium used. Actual costs when individual securities are used include both known and unknown factors. Even the known factors, which include brokerage commissions, odd-lot fees and taxes, vary with the price of the specific shares and the total amount of money involved. The unknown factors include the difference between the closing price on the date indicated for the transaction and the price at which it could actually take place, which might be higher or lower and again would depend in part upon the type of security and the size of the fund.

Expenses in general are apt to be proportionate to the profits derived from a formula plan. The larger the profits, the larger the total costs of transactions, but the portion of the profits which should be mentally set aside to cover expenses is more or less constant. Estimates indicate that the maximum ratio of expenses to profits is around 15%.

A point to be kept in mind on expenses is that when a plan calls for fairly frequent switches between stocks and bonds, only a small portion of the total fund is usually involved. During the course of a long stock market rise, for example, the stock portion might be decreased from 80% to 20% of the total in a series of half a dozen transactions. But the total amount transferred is no greater than if it were transferred in one major switch at the top.

8. *Income Estimates*

Income on the stock portion of the hypothetical funds can be computed fairly easily, since the actual income record of the Dow-Jones industrials is readily available. The difficulty in making comparisons between income under a plan and income without a plan lies in the two additional assumptions that are necessary: (1) how the bond portion is invested and (2) how the money would otherwise have been invested. Where estimates are given in this book, the comparatively low return of 2% is assumed for the bond portion, on the theory that this is a conservative rate for a fund partially invested in highest-grade bonds and partially held in savings accounts for quick availability when stock purchases are made.

Comparisons are given with the corresponding income on the starting amount of money fully invested throughout the period in common stocks, and for a similar fund divided equally between stocks and bonds. The reader can decide for himself which comparison seems the more realistic.

9. *Prices*

In plans which call for a purchase or sale at a specific market level, it is assumed in the tests that the transaction took place at that precise level and that it could have been made if it fell within the day's high and low. (The latter point is of significance only in the case of a particular plan which called for purchases at 98.4 in March, 1938, when the lowest closing was 98.95 but the low for the day was 97.46.) If, instead of using the figure called for by the plan, the closing price for the day or the following day had been used, the results in most cases would have been improved, since purchases were usually made in falling markets and sales in rising markets.

Where the plans call for action at the end of three-month periods or years, the closing price is used. In these cases, a small margin was allowed between the required level of the index and the actual figure for the market. The rule used was a maximum of 1%. It made no difference except in a very few cases, but on the basis of the hypothetical tests it would appear to be a reasonable addition to any plan of this type.

## CHAPTER VIII

### THE CONSTANT DOLLAR FUND

"IT'S WHAT you *keep* that counts," declared one of the sages of Wall Street a number of years ago. The Constant Dollar Fund type of plan is simply a practical way of following this eminently sound advice. It is probably the simplest of all plans to follow and is especially suited for investors who prefer not to be bothered with mathematical computations or frequent changes in the division of their investment fund between stocks and bonds.

The basic idea, as the name indicates, is to hold the market value of the stock investment relatively steady, by selling stocks as prices go up and buying them as prices go down. In effect, as stock prices rise, all profits are taken and invested in bonds or otherwise salted away so as to be available for use in buying stocks back at lower levels. All that is necessary to formulate a plan is to decide how frequently or under what conditions profits are to be taken or re-investments made. There are numerous possible methods.

Regardless of the method chosen, a Constant Dollar Fund, like all other formula plans, requires an initial division into a bond fund and a stock fund. Whatever dollar amount is decided upon at the start for the common stock portion is the controlling figure for operation under the plan.

From then on, the simplest method of all is to make adjustments only at specified time intervals, such as six months or a year. Depending upon whether stock prices go up or down, stocks are automatically sold or bought each six or 12 months in sufficient quantity to bring the dollar amount of stock investment, at then current market values, down or up to the starting amount.

To illustrate, assume that a $20,000 total fund is involved, and that it is initially decided to invest half the fund in stocks and half in high-grade bonds, and to make necessary adjustments only at the end of each year. The stock fund is set, therefore, at $10,000. At the end of a year, the market value of the stocks held is calculated; if it is less than $10,000, the amount necessary to bring it up to this figure is transferred from the bond account to the stock account; if it is more than $10,000, sufficient stocks are sold to bring the figure down to $10,000 and the proceeds are invested in bonds. At each succeeding year-end, the same process is repeated.

The effect of this procedure is that profits are taken as prices rise and additional money is invested as prices decline. Table 2 shows how an investment fund would have fared if this extremely

TABLE 2

CONSTANT DOLLAR FUND

Result of Maintaining Constant $10,000 Fund 1937–1946
Adjustments Made at End of Each Calendar Year

| Date | D-J Ind. average | Stock fnud | Bond fund | Value of total fund |
|---|---|---|---|---|
| Dec. 31, 1936 | 180 | $10,000 | $10,000 | $20,000 |
| Dec. 31, 1937 | 120.8 | 6,710 | 10,000 | 16,710 |
| Increase stock fund to $10,000 | 120.8 | 10,000 | 6,710 | 16,710 |
| Dec. 31, 1938 | 154.8 | 12,815 | 6,710 | 19,525 |
| Reduce stock fund to $10,000 | 154.8 | 10,000 | 9,525 | 19,525 |
| Dec. 31, 1939 | 150.2 | 9,700 | 9,525 | 19,225 |
| Increase stock fund to $10,000 | 150.2 | 10,000 | 9,225 | 19,225 |
| Dec. 31, 1940 | 131.1 | 8,730 | 9,225 | 17,955 |
| Increase stock fund to $10,000 | 131.1 | 10,000 | 7,955 | 17,955 |
| Dec. 31, 1941 | 111.0 | 8,465 | 7,955 | 16,420 |
| Increase stock fund to $10,000 | 111.0 | 10,000 | 6,420 | 16,420 |
| Dec. 31, 1942 | 119.4 | 10,755 | 6,420 | 17,175 |
| Reduce stock fund to $10,000 | 119.4 | 10,000 | 7,175 | 17,175 |
| Dec. 31, 1943 | 135.9 | 11,380 | 7,175 | 18,555 |
| Reduce stock fund to $10,000 | 135.9 | 10,000 | 8,555 | 18,555 |
| Dec. 31, 1944 | 152.3 | 11,205 | 8,555 | 19,760 |
| Reduce stock fund to $10,000 | 152.3 | 10,000 | 9,760 | 19,760 |
| Dec. 31, 1945 | 192.9 | 12,665 | 9,760 | 22,425 |
| Reduce stock fund to $10,000 | 192.9 | 10,000 | 12,425 | 22,425 |
| Dec. 31, 1946 | 180 | 9,330 | 12,425 | 21,755 |

simple method had been followed from 1937 through 1946, assuming that the stocks held moved exactly as the Dow-Jones industrial average did and that there was no fluctuation in the market value of the bonds held. Since the average stood at the same level at the end as at the start, there would have been neither gain nor loss in the fund if it had remained fully invested through the ten years. Maintaining a constant dollar fund, however, resulted in a gain of $1,755 (before allowance for expenses of making transactions). This result is not spectacular—it is about 1¾% a year on the amount invested in stocks or ⅞% a year on the entire fund—but practically no effort or attention would have been required to achieve it. Furthermore, if a class of securities which normally moves up and down faster than the Dow-Jones industrials had been used, the result would have been considerably better.

The Constant Dollar Fund method can be modified in numerous ways, described later. But since its chief virtue is its complete simplicity, let us first explore the possibilities of a long-term plan which requires nothing more than a yearly valuation of the fund.

The first point to consider is whether the adjustment between stocks and bonds should be made annually, regardless of whether or not stock prices have moved up or down very much during the preceding year. The method has the advantage of being purely automatic, but at times it results in selling stocks much too soon in a bull market and buying them too early in a bear market.

This difficulty can be partially overcome by setting a minimum percentage that stocks must rise or fall from the level of the preceding adjustment in order to require the next transfer from bonds to stocks or vice versa. A convenient set of percentages to use, which would have proved satisfactory in the past for a long-term program, is a 25% advance—20% decline combination. Thus, if a plan were started when the market index stood at 150, no adjustment would be made until the first year-end at which the index was above 187 or below 120. If the investor prefers not to bother referring to a market index or average, he can simply wait until the total market value of his common stocks rises 25% or falls 20%. In practice, the investor taking action only at year-ends would probably wish to do so if the market were reasonably close to the required level and in the hypothetical tests a lee-way of about 1 percentage point has been permitted.

If this rule is added to the hypothetical plan from 1937 to 1946, the adjustments at the ends of 1939, 1940, 1942 and 1943 would have been omitted, and the final value for a $20,000 fund would have been about $22,400. The gain over the simple plan was thus about $650, or about 35% additional profit.

The longer a Constant Dollar plan is followed, and the better it works, the smaller the ratio of stocks to the total fund will become. This is because the stock portion is intentionally held at the same figure, while the total fund increases in size. In the example given, the stock fund was 50% of the total at the start, but only about 45% at the end of ten years, at the same level of the market. This is not a serious decrease, but over a longer period of time, especially if price fluctuations became more violent, the stock fund might easily decline to 25% or even less.

A provision for automatically increasing the Constant Dollar figure occasionally is therefore desirable. But it is important not to increase the figure when stock prices are near a top. A reasonably safe rule is to increase the stock fund only at a time when the plan calls for the *purchase* of stocks. This at least insures that it will not be done at the worst possible time. It is also usually desirable not to increase the stock fund too fast, especially if there has been a long upward trend preceding the decline signalling the purchase.

The following rule for automatically increasing the Constant Dollar figure in a fund that started off half stocks and half bonds would have worked reasonably well, if combined with annual adjustments after a 25% rise or 20% decline in the Dow-Jones industrials, over the entire 50 years from 1897 to 1946 and would fit almost any conceivable circumstances:

CHART 3 HYPOTHETICAL CONSTANT DOLLAR FUND 1897–1946

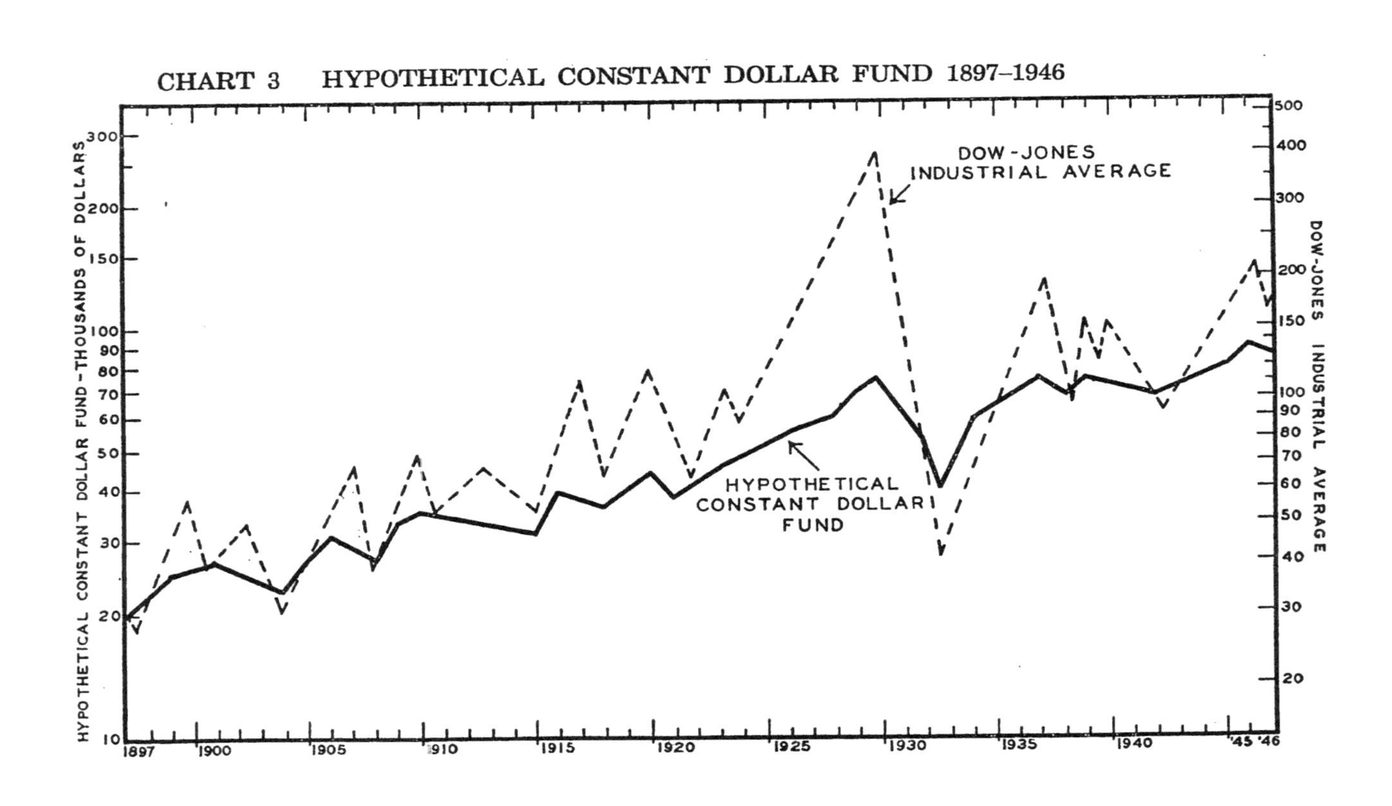

When a *purchase* of stocks is required, compute the ratio of the existing Constant Dollar figure to the total market value of the entire fund. If it is more than 40%, adjust the stock fund to the figure previously used; if it is 40% or less, increase the Constant Dollar figure as follows:

1. If the ratio is between 35% and 40%, increase the Stock fund to 50% of the total;
2. If the ratio is between 30% and 35%, increase the Stock fund to 40% of the total;
3. If the ratio is between 25% and 30%, increase the Stock fund to 35% of the total.

If the stock fund is initially more than 50% of the total fund, or less than 50%, different sets of percentages would have to be used, but the same general idea could easily be followed.

The annual Constant Dollar Fund plan, modified by the rule to await a 25% advance or 20% decline and the provisions for increasing the Stock fund, was applied to the Dow-Jones industrial average from 1897 through 1946 and the results are shown graphically in Chart 3. The starting fund was $20,000, divided equally into $10,000 of stocks and $10,000 of bonds. The Constant Stock figure remained at $10,000 from 1897 until December 31, 1907. On that date the value of the entire fund was $27,000 and a purchase was called for. A $10,000 stock fund would then have been 37% of the total, so the "constant" figure was increased to 50% of $27,000, or $13,500. The stock figure was subsequently raised to $18,100 at the end of 1917, to $21,500 at the end of 1930, to $27,000 at the end of 1937, and to $33,500 at the end of 1941.

A test covering the 50 years from 1897 to 1946 places any formula plan at a disadvantage, because the industrial average was about 500% higher at the end than at the beginning of the period. Few plans can do as well under such circumstances as a "buy and hold" program in common stocks alone, because a plan requires part of the fund to be in bonds at practically all times and because profits are cut short as stock prices rise.

In this case, the 1946 closing value of $85,730 compares with about $120,000 if the original $20,000 could have been placed in the Dow-Jones industrials back in 1897 and left there. If $10,000 had been invested in stocks and $10,000 in bonds without the plan, the final value would have been about $70,000.

Despite this moderate long-term result, the investor who is interested in the simplest possible plan will find the details of the comparison worth studying. He should note particularly the growth from about 1925 to 1946, compared with the market average, and from 1936 to 1946. As with all plans, he should compare it with his actual investment results in the same period.

The Constant Dollar Fund has one major disadvantage. That is the fact that it cannot, or should not, be adopted without some reference to the level of security prices at the time. While, as Chart 3 shows, the investor who had adopted a Constant Dollar plan several years prior to 1929, for instance, would have fared reasonably well in the period following (because he had had time to build up his bond portion to a substantial amount), an investor who started such a plan in 1929 would have experienced considerable difficulty unless he had started off with a small stock fund and a large bond fund.

It is not necessary to worry about how *high* stock prices may go, under a Constant Dollar plan. But it is essential for the conservative investor to make some estimate of how *low* they may go, and to provide enough money in the bond fund to take care of purchases down to that level. For example, an investor with a $20,000 fund who was starting a Constant Dollar plan when the industrial average was around 200 might calculate it this way:

> If stock prices should decline immediately and he starts with a $10,000 stock fund, each 20% drop will make it necessary to transfer $2,000 (20% of $10,000) from bonds to stocks. Assuming that his stocks move with the average,

that would mean successive transfers of $2,000 at 160, 128, 102 and 82. (If he is making adjustments only at year-ends, the amount needed should be lower; this calculation gives him his maximum requirement.) He happens to feel that 100 is about as low as the industrial average is likely to go, or at least to stay for any length of time, so he can see that his bond fund is unlikely to drop below $4,000. This he finds a satisfactory figure.

If, on the other hand, he were starting with the market index at 400, his possible purchase points would be 320; 256; 205; 164; 131 and 105. The risk of his bond fund becoming exhausted would be much greater and a starting stock fund less than half of the total would seem advisable. Furthermore, if the stocks he was using moved faster than the industrial average, he would need to use greater caution even starting at the 200 level.

To this extent, the Constant Dollar Fund requires a market forecast. No formula plan is completely ideal, however, and the utter simplicity of the Constant Dollar operation has recommended it to certain types of investors.

---

The remainder of this chapter discusses the mathematical basis of the Constant Dollar Fund and several somewhat more complicated methods of applying the principle which would, in the past, have produced greater capital appreciation than the very simple form already described.

The first possibility is to ignore the calendar altogether and base adjustments upon simple percentage rises and declines: when stock prices go up, say 25%, sell out enough stocks to reduce the market value of those retained to the starting figure. If stocks decline 20% (the percent drop which is the equivalent of a 25% rise in number of points), buy enough stocks to build up the stock account to its initial amount. If this procedure is followed, and stocks first rise 25% and then decline 20%, this is the result:

| | Stock prices | Stocks | Bonds | Total |
|---|---|---|---|---|
| Original fund | 100 | $10,000 | $10,000 | $20,000 |
| Stocks rise 25% | 125 | 12,500 | 10,000 | 22,500 |
| | *Sell stocks and buy bonds* | | | |
| | 125 | 10,000 | 12,500 | 22,500 |
| Stocks decline 20% | 100 | 8,000 | 12,500 | 20,500 |

The net profit on the "round trip" in this case is $500. The proportion—2½% on the entire fund or 5% on the initial stock investment—will hold true for any 25%-rise-and-20%-decline or 20%-decline-and-25%-rise, regardless of market level.

Smaller or larger percentages than these might be used. Higher percentage intervals result in greater profits: two 25% advances followed by two 20% declines would produce a total profit of 10% on the stock fund, whereas a single 50% rise followed by a 33⅓% decline would increase the stock fund by 16.7%. However, the more frequent occurrence of smaller fluctuations generally makes the use of somewhat smaller percentages more advantageous.

For the industrial average, past records indicate that 20% advances and 16.7% declines are likely to be the most satisfactory percentages. A round trip of these dimensions produces a 3.3% profit on the stock fund. If stocks which move faster than the average are used, but transactions are made only when the average has advanced 20% or declined 16.7%, the profit will be considerably greater.

Table 3 shows the results of applying this method to the industrial average from 1937 through 1946. The starting level was 180, which became the figure on which the entire schedule is based. The first sell point above that would have been 120% of 180, or 216, which was never reached. Purchase points below 180 were 150, 125 and 104⅛. These subsequently became selling points on the way up.

## TABLE 3

## CONSTANT DOLLAR FUND

RESULT OF MAINTAINING CONSTANT $10,000 FUND 1937–1946
CHANGES MADE AFTER EVERY 20% ADVANCE OR 16.7% DECLINE

| Date | D-J Ind. average | Stock fund | Bond fund | Value of total fund |
|---|---|---|---|---|
| Jan., 1937 | 180 | $10,000 | $10,000 | $20,000 |
| *Stocks decline 16.7%* | | | | |
| Sept., 1937 | 150 | 8,333 | 10,000 | 18,333 |
| Increase stock fund to $10,000 | 150 | 10,000 | 8,333 | 18,333 |
| *Stocks decline 16.7%* | | | | |
| Nov., 1937 | 125 | 8,333 | 8,333 | 16,666 |
| Increase stock fund to $10,000 | 125 | 10,000 | 6,666 | 16,666 |
| *Stocks decline 16.7%* | | | | |
| March, 1938 | 104⅛ | 8,334 | 6,666 | 15,000 |
| Increase stock fund to $10,000 | 104⅛ | 10,000 | 5,000 | 15,000 |
| *Stocks rise 20%* | | | | |
| June, 1938 | 125 | 12,000 | 5,000 | 17,000 |
| Reduce stock fund to $10,000 | 125 | 10,000 | 7,000 | 17,000 |
| *Stocks rise 20%* | | | | |
| Oct., 1938 | 150 | 12,000 | 7,000 | 19,000 |
| Reduce stock fund to $10,000 | 150 | 10,000 | 9,000 | 19,000 |
| *Stocks decline 16.7%* | | | | |
| April, 1939 | 125 | 8,333 | 9,000 | 17,333 |
| Increase stock fund to $10,000 | 125 | 10,000 | 7,333 | 17,333 |
| *Stocks rise 20%* | | | | |
| Sept., 1939 | 150 | 12,000 | 7,333 | 19,333 |
| Reduce stock fund to $10,000 | 150 | 10,000 | 9,333 | 19,333 |
| *Stocks decline 16.7%* | | | | |
| May, 1940 | 125 | 8,333 | 9,333 | 17,666 |
| Increase stock fund to $10,000 | 125 | 10,000 | 7,666 | 17,666 |
| *Stocks decline 16.7%* | | | | |
| March, 1942 | 104⅛ | 8,334 | 7,666 | 16,000 |
| Increase stock fund to $10,000 | 104⅛ | 10,000 | 6,000 | 16,000 |
| *Stocks rise 20%* | | | | |
| Jan., 1943 | 125 | 12,000 | 6,000 | 18,000 |
| Reduce stock fund to $10,000 | 125 | 10,000 | 8,000 | 18,000 |
| *Stocks rise 20%* | | | | |
| July, 1944 | 150 | 12,000 | 8,000 | 20,000 |
| Reduce stock fund to $10,000 | 150 | 10,000 | 10,000 | 20,000 |
| *Stocks rise 20%* | | | | |
| Sept., 1945 | 180 | 12,000 | 10,000 | 22,000 |
| Reduce stock fund to $10,000 | 180 | 10,000 | 12,000 | 22,000 |
| Value, Dec. 31, 1946 | 180 | 10,000 | 12,000 | 22,000 |

Two more transactions were called for than under the simplest annual method and the end result is slightly better—a gain of $2,000 on a $10,000 stock fund for the ten years. It is also obvious, on the other hand, that some purchases were made too early after a decline started and some sales too soon after a rise got under way. By sacrificing a few of the minor fluctuations, better results can be obtained if a provision for delaying action is added to the plan.

One method is to make transactions only at specified time intervals (but shorter than a full year) and then only when the market has in the meantime moved up or down the specified percentage. An interval of three months appears to be a convenient one for this purpose—a much shorter time is apt to provide insufficient delay, while a longer waiting period may result in missing too many transactions. The same type of schedule can be used as in the preceding example. The difference lies in waiting for the regular quarterly date before making any transaction, only making it then if the market average is still above or below the significant point (as the case may be), or within 1% of it. Occasionally the delay will cause a transaction to be missed, but more often it results in a better price and once in a while, as in late 1937, a second action level is reached before any purchase or sale is made. During the ten-year testing period, the 1939 purchase and sale would have been missed completely, but every other transaction would have been made at a more favorable price by waiting to the end of the quarter. The end result would have been a $2,745 over-all gain on a $10,000 stock fund, compared with a $2,000 gain on the same schedule when the transactions were made immediately.

Another delaying method, which can be combined with any of the preceding plans, is based on an assumption that when the trend of the market changes direction, the new trend will continue for some minimum distance, and that, therefore, no transactions should be made until that percentage rise or decline is completed.

There have been few major market movements over the past 50 years which did not carry the industrial average up at least 50% or down at least 33⅓%. To use this form of delaying action the investor computes the figure which would be 50% above the lowest level reached by the market average, or 33⅓% below the highest. This will be his first selling or buying level. When it is reached, he computes a new schedule for additional sales or purchases, building it on the level at which his first sale or purchase took place.

Table 4 shows the application of this method to a $10,000

TABLE 4

CONSTANT DOLLAR FUND

RESULT OF MAINTAINING CONSTANT $10,000 FUND 1937–1946

ADJUSTMENTS MADE AT END OF QUARTER AFTER 20% ADVANCE OR 16.7% DECLINE, EXCEPT AFTER CHANGE OF TREND, WHEN FIRST ADJUSTMENT POSTPONED UNTIL 50% ADVANCE OR 33.3% DECLINE

| Date | D-J Ind. Average | Stock fund | Bond fund | Value of total fund |
|---|---|---|---|---|
| Dec. 31, 1936 | 180.0 | $10,000 | $10,000 | $20,000 |
| *Stocks decline 33.3% from 194.4 high (129.7)* | | | | |
| Dec. 31, 1937 | 120.8 | 6,710 | 10,000 | 16,710 |
| Increase stock fund to $10,000 | 120.8 | 10,000 | 6,710 | 16,710 |
| *Stocks decline additional 16.7% (100.6)* | | | | |
| March 31, 1938 | 98.9 | 8,185 | 6,710 | 14,895 |
| Increase stock fund to $10,000 | 98.9 | 10,000 | 4,895 | 14,895 |
| *Stocks rise 50% from 98.9 low (148.4)* | | | | |
| Dec. 31, 1938 | 154.8 | 15,650 | 4,895 | 20,545 |
| Reduce stock fund to $10,000 | 154.8 | 10,000 | 10,545 | 20,545 |
| *Stocks decline 33.3% from 158.4 high (105.6)* | | | | |
| March 31, 1942 | 99.5 | 6,430 | 10,545 | 16,975 |
| Increase stock fund to $10,000 | 99.5 | 10,000 | 6,975 | 16,975 |
| *Stocks rise 50% from 92.9 low (139.4)* | | | | |
| June 30, 1943 | 143.4 | 14,410 | 6,975 | 21,385 |
| Reduce stock fund to $10,000 | 143.4 | 10,000 | 11,385 | 21,385 |
| *Stocks rise additional 20% (172.1)* | | | | |
| Sept. 30, 1945 | 181.7 | 12,670 | 11,385 | 24,055 |
| Reduce stock fund to $10,000 | 181.7 | 10,000 | 14,055 | 24,055 |
| *Stocks rise additional 20% (206.5)* | | | | |
| June 30, 1946 | 205.6* | 11,315 | 14,055 | 25,370 |
| Reduce stock fund to $10,000 | 205.6 | 10,000 | 15,370 | 25,370 |
| Value Dec. 31, 1946 | 180.0 | 8,755 | 15,370 | 24,125 |

*An application of rule that action is taken when average is within 1% of required level.

stock fund where transactions were also made only at the ends of calendar quarters. The number of transactions for the entire ten-year period was reduced to seven, but the total gain was increased to $4,125.

The results of using the several possible variations of the Constant Dollar Fund method during the 1937-1946 testing period compare as follows:

| *Method* | *Description* | *Profit on $10,000 stock fund* |
|---|---|---|
| 1 | Annual adjustments | $1,755 |
| 2 | Simple 20%–16.7% schedule | 2,000 |
| 3 | Same as 2 but transactions only at ends of quarters | 2,745 |
| 4 | Same as 3 but with additional provision to await 50% advance or 33⅓% decline after change in trend | 4,125 |

These results are all based on the use of the industrial average for the stock portion. When the plan is applied to classes of securities which move up and down faster than this predominantly high-grade stock index, some striking improvements in results appear. The following table uses the indexes described in Chapter VII and is based upon a Constant Dollar Fund operated according to Method 4, for the ten years 1937–1946.

| Class of Security | Profit on $10,000 Stock Fund | Lowest Value of $10,000 Bond Fund* |
|---|---|---|
| Dow-Jones industrial average | $4,125 | $4,895 |
| Business Cycle Stocks | 6,835 | 3,505 |
| Low-Priced Stocks | 12,530 | 1,360 |
| Highly Speculative Stocks | 21,345 | 725 |
| Fully Managed Stock Fund | 8,280 | 4,295 |
| Fully Managed Stock Fund without use of plan | $3,150 | $10,000 |

*These figures represent the unused portion of the bond fund after transferring the amount required to bring the stock fund up to $10,000 on March 31, 1938.

## Effect on Income

Investment income under the Constant Dollar Plan would have been higher than on a similar fund without the plan, if it is assumed that the fund would otherwise have been divided equally between stocks and bonds. Using the Dow-Jones industrial average as the stock portion and basing income estimates on actual dividends paid on the stocks and a 2% interest rate on the bond portion, income on a total fund of $20,000 for the 1937–1946 period would have compared as follows:

A. Under Constant Dollar Plan, Method 4

| | |
|---|---|
| Income on Stocks | $4,708 |
| Income on Bonds | 2,045 |
| Total income | $6,753 |

B. On fund divided equally between stocks and bonds, with no changes during 10-year period

| | |
|---|---|
| Income on Stocks | $3,776 |
| Income on Bonds | 2,000 |
| Total income | $5,776 |

Income under the plan was lower than it would have been if the entire fund had been invested in stocks and no changes made. On that basis, total income would have amounted to $7,551.

## CONCLUSION

Any of the preceding versions of the Constant Dollar Fund has the same major disadvantage as the very simple annual method already discussed; namely, the danger of starting the plan at too high a market level and providing insufficient funds for buying additional stocks as prices decline. Possible means of coping with this problem have also been described earlier in the chapter.

As compared with other types of formula plans, the Constant Dollar Fund is considered primarily because of its simplicity. It is neither as free from a market forecast as the Constant. Stock-Bond Ratio plan nor as potentially profitable as the Variable Stock-Bond Ratio. But its simplicity is hard to surpass.

# CHAPTER IX

## The Constant Stock-Bond Ratio

There is one type of formula plan—and so far as is known, only one type—which neither involves any forecast of future market range nor depends upon past history repeating itself. It is equally adaptable to any general level of the market and the only requirement for its continued operation is that stock prices fluctuate at least moderately.

This is the simple Constant Stock-Bond Ratio, or "equalizing," type of plan. It is far from ideal either as a producer of maximum capital growth or, in some respects, as a protective device against depreciation in a falling market. But many investors have found this type of plan well adapted for investment funds in which relative capital safety and steady income are the sole objectives. The plan will operate to *prevent* mistakes in judgment which might otherwise result in capital loss, and the small capital increase resulting from the plan (usually averaging about 1% a year in investment-grade common stocks) can, if desired, be regarded as additional income.

Simple Constant Ratio type plans have been in actual use by some investors for a long enough period of time to provide a good indication of the type of results which can be expected. A particularly interesting example is provided by an Ohio investment counsellor who has been connected with the operation of an institutional fund of about $1,000,000 started in 1935. In this case, not only is the experience of the fund since adoption of an informal plan in 1938 available, but also the experience of the fund without any plan during the three preceding years. The record points up the importance of judging any formula plan result, not in comparison with a buy-and-hold program, but with the actual result achieved without a plan.

The experience of this Ohio fund has been expressed in the form of index numbers and is compared with a "normal expectation." The latter is simply the theoretical experience of a fund holding 60% cash and 40% invested in the Dow-Jones industrial average as of July 1, 1935, when the actual fund was started. The records of the fund, before and after adoption of the plan, and the "normal expectation" are pictured in Chart 4.

## CHART 4

EXPERIENCE OF INSTITUTIONAL FUND, BEFORE AND AFTER ADOPTION OF SIMPLE CONSTANT RATIO PLAN

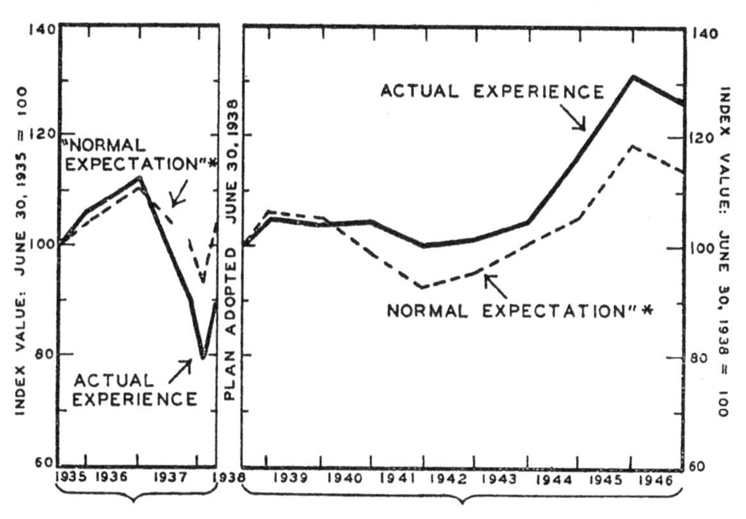


Before Adoption of Plan After Adoption of Plan

*Theoretical experience of a fund holding 60% cash and 40% invested in the Dow-Jones industrial average.

From July 1, 1935, to July 1, 1938, the "normal expectation" would have been a 5.30% increase in market value of the fund. But the actual experience was a decline of 10.85%, or a loss of 16.15% of principal in three years in relation to the "normal expectation." At this point the Investment Committee took a backward look and observed that "it had unconsciously been drawn into purchase of equities at the high levels of the 1937 market and sales at subsequent lower levels."

As a defense against making the same mistakes again in the future, the Committee on June 30, 1938, adopted the simple plan of limiting investment in stocks (including preferreds) to 50% of the market value of the portfolio and adjusting the portfolio back to this figure whenever there was any marked variation from this percentage. During the eight and one-half years of operation under this simple formula, necessary adjustments proved to be small and infrequent, but consistently in the right direction. And by the end of 1946 the value of the principal, as compared with the date the plan was adopted, had increased by 26.74%, or nearly twice the "normal expectation" of a 13.92% increase. For the period of the plan, income averaged 4.48% a year.

The basic nature of the Constant Stock-Bond Ratio plan has probably become clear already from the preceding illustration. The plan consists simply of determining a set proportion of a total fund which is to be invested in common stocks or equity-type securities, and then maintaining that ratio by readjusting the holdings whenever prices move enough to disturb it appreciably. The original ratio can be whatever is considered most suitable for the particular fund—one-third stocks, half stocks, or even more.

A simple example illustrates why this maintenance of a "constant ratio" is bound to result in a small profit whenever stock prices go up and then down, or down and then up, by a sufficient amount to bring the plan into action. Assume that an investment fund starts off divided half in stocks and half in high-grade bonds and that there is no fluctuation at all in the latter. It is decided that enough stocks will be sold and bonds bought to make the two equal again after stock prices rise by 25%. Or if prices go down by 20%, the process will be reversed—bonds will be sold and stocks bought. This is the way it would work if a $20,000 fund were started on this basis:

| | Stock Prices | Stocks | % of Fund | Bonds | % of Fund | Total Fund |
|---|---|---|---|---|---|---|
| Original fund......... | 100 | $10,000 | 50% | $10,000 | 50% | $20,000 |
| After stocks rise 25% . | 125 | 12,500 | 55.6 | 10,000 | 44.4 | 22,500 |
| Sell enough stocks and buy bonds to restore original | | | | | | |
| 50%–50% ratio ..... | 125 | 11,250 | 50% | 11,250 | 50% | 22,500 |
| Stocks return to starting point, | | | | | | |
| a decline of 20% ...... | 100 | 9,000 | 44.4 | 11,250 | 55.6 | 20,250 |

If, instead of rising and then declining, the stocks first declined 20% and then rose to the starting point, with a readjustment to the 50–50 ratio at the bottom, the result would have been exactly the same. Thus:

| | Stock Prices | Stocks | % of Fund | Bonds | % of Fund | Total Fund |
|---|---|---|---|---|---|---|
| Original fund......... | 100 | $10,000 | 50% | $10,000 | 50% | $20,000 |
| After stocks decline 20% | 80 | 8,000 | 44.4 | 10,000 | 55.6 | 18,000 |
| Sell enough bonds and buy stocks to restore original | | | | | | |
| 50%–50% ratio ...... | 80 | 9,000 | 50% | 9,000 | 50% | 18,000 |
| Stocks return to starting point, | | | | | | |
| a rise of 25%......... | 100 | 11,250 | 55.6 | 9,000 | 44.4 | 20,250 |

## Mathematical Basis

Similarities and differences between this Constant Ratio operation and the Constant Dollar Fund described in the preceding chapter are such that a comparison of the two is made at this point to facilitate the reader's understanding of the mathematics involved. However, it is not essential to understand *why* a plan works in order to profit from its use; non-mathematicians who find the explanation difficult to follow can safely ignore it.

The Constant Dollar operation, it will be recalled, resulted in the taking of the *entire* profit on stocks which existed when the action point was reached. In the Constant Ratio type of operation, only *part* of the profit is taken and transferred to bonds. If the ratio is 50–50, then half of the profit is taken out of stocks. If the ratio is 25% stocks—75% bonds, then 75% of the profit is taken, or if it is 75% stocks—25% bonds, only 25% of the profit is taken. The proportion of the profit which is transferred from the stock account to the bond account will always be the same as the percentage of the fund held in the defensive side.

With either type of plan, the profit on a completed "round-trip" is simply the loss that is avoided on the *profit taken out of stocks*. In the first example above, $1,250 of profit was taken out of stocks and placed in stable securities. Stocks then declined 20%. The loss avoided on the $1,250 profit was thus 20% or $250, which is the amount of gain indicated for the entire "round-trip." The process is simply reversed when the decline comes before the gain.

Because the entire profit is taken out of stocks in the Constant Dollar plan, instead of only part as in the Constant Ratio, the round-trip gain is bound to be greater, all other things being equal. An example in the preceding chapter similar in every other detail to that given above resulted in a $500 profit, or twice the result for the Constant Ratio plan. The reason is obvious, for the profit taken out of stocks was twice as great in one case as in the other. The Constant Ratio has certain advantages over the Constant Dollar plan, however, which must be considered before deciding that one plan is preferable to the other.

The chief practical application of this arithmetic is in the decision as to what the bond-stock relationship under a Constant Ratio plan should be. The purpose and requirements of the particular investment fund should of course be the controlling consideration. If stability is important, the stock proportion should be fairly low; if inflation protection is desired, it might be fairly high. But for capital growth, certain ratios work better than others, solely because of the mathematics involved.

From the point of view of potential profit on the entire fund (including the bond portion as well as the amount invested in stocks), the ratio which gives the highest profit on a "round-trip" is 50% stocks—50% bonds. In relation to the common stock investment by itself, however, the smaller the proportion of common stocks to the total fund, the higher the percentage profit. The reason for this can be seen by considering what would happen if a fund were divided into 10% stocks and 90% bonds. When an adjustment was made after a rise, 90% of the profit would be taken out of stocks, only 10% left to be subject to a following decline. It would actually be quite similar to a Constant Dollar Fund type of plan.

For a "round-trip" consisting of a 50% advance and a 33⅓% decline—with a readjustment only at the extreme points—the percentage profit on the stock fund alone and on the entire fund, with various proportions of the fund invested in stocks, would be as follows:

| Fund divided | | % profit after 50% advance and 33⅓% decline on | |
|---|---|---|---|
| Stocks | Bonds | Stock Fund | Entire Fund |
| 10% | 90% | 15% | 1.5% |
| 20 | 80 | 13.4 | 2.7 |
| 30 | 70 | 11.7 | 3.5 |
| 40 | 60 | 10.0 | 4.0 |
| 50 | 50 | 8.3 | 4.2 |
| 60 | 40 | 6.7 | 4.0 |
| 70 | 30 | 5.0 | 3.5 |
| 80 | 20 | 3.3 | 2.7 |
| 90 | 10 | 1.7 | 1.5 |

It must be emphasized that these figures and conclusions are based upon ending market levels no higher than those at the start. In any upward trend period, greatest profits will be shown by the fund with the highest proportion of stock investment; in a downward trend, the lowest stock investment will show the best result.

## Operating Details and Results

The practical operation of an investment fund under a Constant Ratio plan is not very different from that described for a Constant Dollar Fund in the preceding chapter and the same variations and delaying provisions can be used. Adjustments can be made simply on a calendar basis, or they can be made whenever the market goes up or down by some pre-determined percentage, or a combination of the two can be used, as suggested for a Constant Dollar Fund, by making adjustments on quarterly dates *if* stocks have moved up or down a specified percentage. To this can be added a provision to wait after a change in trend for a one-third decline or 50% advance from the highest or lowest point previously reached.

The actual adjustment, however, requires a little more computation than under a Constant Dollar plan, where the only necessary figure is the difference between the current market value of stocks held and the amount decided upon for the stock fund. With the Constant Ratio it is necessary to figure the market value of the stock fund, the value of the total fund, and then compute the dollar amount which would be the required stock proportion at prevailing stock prices. The difference between this figure and the value of stocks held is the value of stocks to be bought or sold at that point. Thus, if stocks held were found to be worth $15,000 and the bond fund was valued at $20,000, the total would be $35,000, of which 50% (if that were the required stock ratio) would be $17,500. The difference, or $2,500, would be the value of stocks which should then be purchased to make the fund conform with the plan.

Table 5 shows the hypothetical results for the 1937–1946

TABLE 5

CONSTANT STOCK-BOND RATIO

RESULTS OF MAINTAINING CONSTANT 50—50 RATIO IN $20,000 FUND 1937–1946

A. Using Industrial Average as Stock Portion

| Method | Description | Value of fund Dec. 31, 1946 | Lowest value during 10 years |
|---|---|---|---|
| 1 | Annual adjustments | $20,921 | $14,900 |
| 2 | Simple 20%—16.7% schedule | 21,017 | 14,720 |
| 3 | Same as 2 but transactions only at ends of quarters | 21,424 | 15,195 |
| 4 | Same as 3 but with additional provision to await 50% advance or 33⅓% decline after change in trend | 22,132 | 15,195 |

B. Using Various Types of Securities as Stock Portion and Using Method 4 as Plan

| Class of Security | Value of fund Dec. 31, 1946 | Lowest value during 10 years |
|---|---|---|
| Dow-Jones industrial average | $22,132 | $15,195 |
| Business Cycle Stocks | 23,580 | 13,997 |
| Low-Priced Stocks | 26,877 | 12,270 |
| Highly Speculative Stocks | 31,832 | 11,445 |
| Fully Managed Stock Fund | 26,140 | 14,656 |
| Fully Managed Stock Fund without use of plan | | |
| (a) $10,000 in stocks, $10,000 in bonds | $23,150 | $15,020 |
| (b) $20,000 in stocks | 26,300 | 10,040 |

period of using various possible Constant Ratio plans, and the comparative effects of using securities of varying volatility in connection with the Constant Dollar fund. Much the same variation in results is shown. Complete details for one plan are given in Table 6. Comparison of this with Table 3 in the preceding chapter will clarify the relationship between a Constant Ratio and a Constant Dollar operation.

Income under the Constant Ratio plan during this period would have been lower than on a complete investment in common stocks, but higher than on a fund that was similarly divided into stocks and bonds but in which no changes were made. How much higher or lower depends upon the assumed rate of return on the bond portion. Taking only 2% as average return on the bond portion results in a ten-year figure of $6,347 under Method 4, which compares with $7,551 income on a fully-invested stock fund or $5,776 on a fund half in stocks and half in bonds.

For the particular period used as an example, income works out to a lower figure using the Constant Ratio than that for the Constant Dollar fund. This is principally due to the fact that during most of the period stocks were below the starting level, with the result that stocks held under the Constant Ratio seldom amounted to as much as the $10,000 figure, the amount of stocks held under the Constant Dollar plan. If the reverse had happened, income would have been higher under the Constant Ratio.

The Constant Ratio investor has a choice as to whether he will value his bond account at market or at par value—it has been done both ways by investors using this type of plan. If highest-grade bonds or bank accounts are used, it will obviously make little difference which method is chosen. If lower-grade bonds, whose prices tend to go up and down with those of stocks, are used, valuing the account at market may keep the plan from working as effectively as possible, for if the bonds have declined or risen, too, smaller changes will be required in the stock account. Both to simplify the computations involved and to improve the working of the plan, carrying the bond account at par or "book" value has a good deal to recommend it. But if this is done, it is also wise to keep part of the bond account in savings deposits

TABLE 6

CONSTANT STOCK-BOND RATIO

RESULT OF MAINTAINING 50–50 STOCK-BOND RATIO 1937–1946

Original ratio restored after every 20% advance or 16.7% decline

| Date | D-J Ind. average | Stock fund | Bond fund | Value of total fund |
|---|---|---|---|---|
| Jan., 1937 | 180 | $10,000 | $10,000 | $20,000 |
| *Stocks decline 16.7%* | | | | |
| Sept., 1937 | 150 | 8,333 | 10,000 | 18,333 |
| Sell bonds and buys stocks | 150 | 9,166 | 9,167 | 18,333 |
| *Stocks decline 16.7%* | | | | |
| Nov., 1937 | 125 | 7,638 | 9,167 | 16,805 |
| Sell bonds and buy stocks | 125 | 8,402 | 8,403 | 16,805 |
| *Stocks decline 16.7%* | | | | |
| March, 1938 | 104⅛ | 7,001 | 8,403 | 15,404 |
| Sell bonds and buy stocks | 104⅛ | 7,702 | 7,702 | 15,404 |
| *Stocks rise 20%* | | | | |
| June, 1938 | 125 | 9,242 | 7,702 | 16,944 |
| Sell stocks and buy bonds | 125 | 8,472 | 8,472 | 16,944 |
| *Stocks rise 20%* | | | | |
| Oct., 1938 | 150 | 10,166 | 8,472 | 18,638 |
| Sell stocks and buy bonds | 150 | 9,319 | 9,319 | 18,638 |
| *Stocks decline 16.7%* | | | | |
| April, 1939 | 125 | 7,765 | 9,319 | 17,084 |
| Sell bonds and buy stocks | 125 | 8,542 | 8,542 | 17,084 |
| *Stocks rise 20%* | | | | |
| Sept., 1939 | 150 | 10,250 | 8,542 | 18,792 |
| Sell stocks and buy bonds | 150 | 9,396 | 9,396 | 18,792 |
| *Stocks decline 16.7%* | | | | |
| May, 1940 | 125 | 7,830 | 9,396 | 17,226 |
| Sell bonds and buy stocks | 125 | 8,613 | 8,613 | 17,226 |
| *Stocks decline 16.7%* | | | | |
| March, 1942 | 104⅛ | 7,177 | 8,613 | 15,790 |
| Sell bonds and buy stocks | 104⅛ | 7,895 | 7,895 | 15,790 |
| *Stocks rise 20%* | | | | |
| Jan., 1943 | 125 | 9,474 | 7,895 | 17,369 |
| Sell stocks and buy bonds | 125 | 8,684 | 8,685 | 17,369 |
| *Stocks rise 20%* | | | | |
| July, 1944 | 150 | 10,421 | 8,685 | 19,106 |
| Sell stocks and buy bonds | 150 | 9,553 | 9,553 | 19,106 |
| *Stocks rise 20%* | | | | |
| Sept., 1945 | 180 | 11,464 | 9,553 | 21,017 |
| Sell stocks and buy bonds | 180 | 10,508 | 10,509 | 21,017 |
| Value Dec. 31, 1946 | 180 | 10,508 | 10,509 | 21,017 |

or government bonds which can be liquidated at par when it is necessary to sell bonds and buy stocks.

Certain variations of the Constant Ratio plan, in addition to those already mentioned, have been used by investors operating under the plan. One of the earliest was the use of a business index as a means of delaying purchases until the later stages of a decline. For example, all purchases might be postponed until there is a definite upturn in the Federal Reserve Board Index of Industrial Production. Or, as suggested by H. G. Carpenter in his book, "Investment Timing by Formula Plans," purchases can be postponed until the first month in which the F.R.B. Index declines as little as one point.

As this book is written, stock prices and business have been moving in opposite directions for the better part of two years, and the consequence is a tendency to ignore the possibilities of this method of delaying purchases under a formula plan. It might be noted, however, that reference to a business index would have permitted any purchases required by a formula plan in late 1946 or early 1947, when the Dow-Jones industrial average was at the 165–175 level. The reader who can look back and tell whether that represented the low or only an early stage of the decline which started in the summer of 1946 will be in a better position to decide whether this approach should be investigated further.*

Another variation is the basing of action points upon the value of the fund itself, rather than upon the movements of a stock price index. Following this method, a fund might start with a 50–50 stock bond ratio and not make any change until the stock prices moved up or down sufficiently to change the ratio to 45–55, or 55–45. This method is one of the features of the Yale University Endowment Plan. It has the advantage of making automatic allowance for the fact that stocks held may move

*For an excellent discussion of adaptations of a business index to formula planning, see H. G. Carpenter, "Investment Timing by Formula Plans," Harper & Brothers (1943), pp. 110–113.

more slowly or faster than a market index, and if the bond account is carried at market value, it may provide an additional delaying action—which is an advantage if prices continue to decline but may also result in missing the whole transaction if they don't. (Yale carries its bonds at par for this reason.)

More frequent valuations of the investment fund are necessary under this method—a feature which is no handicap to an institution which would value its portfolio frequently anyway but which might be a considerable nuisance to some individual investors. And it may also detract from the results of superior security selection or the use of fast-moving stocks, by requiring sales too quickly.

A different type of variation in the Constant Ratio plan is the use of different ratios in advancing and declining markets. The Yale Plan (described more fully on page 139) is an example of this. Starting with a 30% stock—70% bond ratio, the Yale Plan provides for no sale of stocks in a rising market until stocks have become 40% of the total fund, when sufficient sales are made to reduce the proportion to 35%. In a falling market, no purchases are made until stocks have declined to 20% of the total fund, when enough are bought to increase the proportion to 25%. If the advance or decline continues, the 35% or 25% ratio is maintained by further sales or purchases whenever 40% or 20% is again reached.

For practical purposes, the Yale Plan primarily consists of a 35%–65% constant ratio in a rising market and a 25%–75% ratio in a declining market. The effect of the two ratios is to postpone sales or purchases until after a very considerable advance or decline. The advantage of this method, however, depends upon extreme fluctuations in common stock prices. To reduce a stock ratio from 35% to 20% (the minimum to bring about a stock purchase) requires a decline of 53%. And to raise the stock ratio from 25% to 40% (the minimum to bring about a sale) takes a 100% advance in prices from the point at which the last purchase was made. (See Chapter VI for a simple method by which these figures can be computed.)

The Yale Plan is designed to fit a very large endowment fund in which income and capital conservation are the only investment objectives. It has operated to prevent mistakes in judgment and as a guide to the proper investment of new money as it comes into the fund. But for smaller funds in which reasonably frequent changes and the prospect of some capital gain from moderate price fluctuations are desired, neither the Yale Plan nor the general method of using different ratios in bull and bear markets appears as good an answer as numerous other possibilities.

The general advantages of the Constant Ratio method lie in its comparative simplicity and its adaptability to whatever future stock price range may develop. There is no danger of ever exhausting the bond fund, no matter how low prices go, nor of being out of stocks, no matter how high. The plan would not become immobilized if the industrial average should for a protracted period fluctuate only—for an extreme example—between 50 and 100, or between 300 and 500. It would not, of course, prevent substantial capital depreciation in the process of the decline to such a low range, nor would it achieve anything like the maximum possible appreciation in an inflationary rise.

Maintaining a constant stock-bond ratio automatically means that profits are taken steadily as prices rise and this reduces profits as compared with those which would be available if stocks were simply bought and held. However, the reduction is less than in any other type of formula plan—if the industrial average *should* rise to the stratosphere, the investor using the Constant Ratio would probably be in a better position than those using any other type of plan.

Even in the extreme 1929–1932 period, a Constant Ratio plan would have worked reasonably well if some form of delaying action had been part of the plan. With a schedule calling for adjustments only at the end of quarters and no action after a change in trend until a 33⅓% decline or 50% advance had been reached, a fund divided 50–50 at the 1929 peak would have

CHART 5 HYPOTHETICAL CONSTANT RATIO FUND 1897–1946

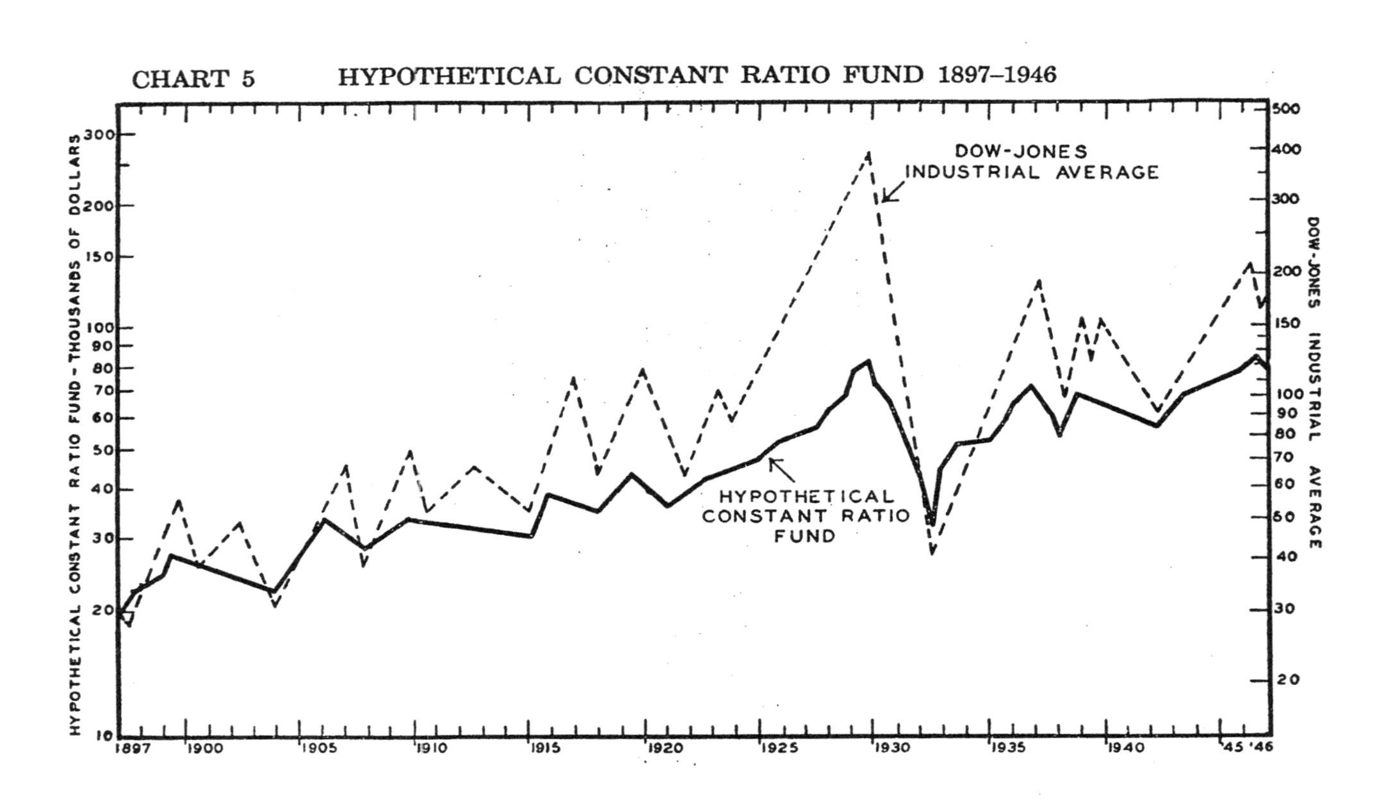

suffered about a 62% capital depreciation at the 1932 low; it would not again have quite reached its 1929 peak value but would have been within 3% of it in June, 1946.

The trend of market value for a hypothetical Constant Ratio fund handled in this fashion (Method 4) for the entire 50 years from 1897 through 1946 is shown in Chart 5.

# CHAPTER X

## INTRODUCTION TO VARIABLE STOCK-BOND RATIO PLANS

FOR AS long as stock market records are available, bull markets have been followed by bear markets, and vice versa. And while the tops and bottoms have come at various levels, as measured by any market index, there is nevertheless a fairly clear pattern that has repeated itself over and over again. Except for the abnormally high 1929 peak and the equally abnormal 1932 low, bull market highs and bear market lows have all fallen within an orderly channel. The top of the band is about 100% above the bottom. (See Chart 6, the Dow-Jones industrial average, page 88.)

If stock prices can be expected to fluctuate in the future more or less according to the general pattern which has existed in the past, then it is possible to develop formula methods of controlling common stock investment which will be both safer and more profitable than the Constant Ratio or Constant Dollar Fund types.

The bad feature of the Constant Ratio plan is that the same proportion of stocks is held at the top of a bull market as is held at the bottom of a bear market. This is an improvement over the buy-and-hold technique, which results in a *higher* proportion being held at the top than at the bottom (because the stocks are worth more), but it is far from a perfect arrangement. Ideally, a plan should call for smaller percentages at the top and larger percentages at the bottom.

Various plans for automatically reducing the proportion of stocks in a rising market and increasing it in a declining one have been developed. All depend basically upon a "variable stock-bond ratio," which simply means that the stock percentage is progressively reduced according to a pre-determined formula as prices go up and is progressively increased as they go down.

Some plans of this nature depend fairly heavily on a continuation of the type of market fluctuations and the long-term (or secular) trend which have existed in the past. Others allow for much wider deviations from historical patterns. It is necessary to understand the mechanics of this type of plan, however, before the significance of these differences can be made clear.

In its simplest form, a schedule can be used which is very similar to that which might be used under a Constant Ratio plan. In order to demonstrate the comparative working of the two methods, this has been done in Table 7. Just as under the simplest Constant Ratio plan, stocks are sold and bonds bought whenever prices rise 20%; bonds are sold and stocks bought whenever prices decline 16.7%. But instead of maintaining the ratio always at 50-50, the ratio is changed by 10 points at each step. The schedule used is:

| Dow-Jones Ind. Average | Stocks | Bonds |
|---|---|---|
| 216 | 30% | 70% |
| 180 | 40 | 60 |
| 150 | 50 | 50 |
| 125 | 60 | 40 |
| 104 | 70 | 30 |

The result can be compared with those of the simple Constant Dollar Fund and Constant Ratio plans as shown in Tables 3 and 6: Constant Dollar Fund—$22,000; Constant Ratio—$21,017; Variable Ratio—$23,387.

*Note to mathematicians:* Just as in the cases of the Constant Ratio and Constant Dollar plans, the final profit is the total of the profits on each "round trip" between two action points. The profit on a "round trip" is the decline avoided in money transferred from stocks to bonds. With a Variable Ratio, *more than the profit* is taken out of the stock portion, which accounts for its greater effectiveness.

The same kinds of delaying actions might be applied to this

very simple Variable Ratio plan as were suggested for the Constant Ratio and Constant Dollar Funds. But the Variable Ratio type of plan introduces certain other problems in plan construction, an understanding of which should precede attempts to work out the most satisfactory form of Variable Ratio plan. The example given above is intended simply as a means of making clear the basic distinctions among the various possibilities in formula planning.

A Variable Ratio plan has to be "anchored" to the market—usually in the form of a market index—in one way or another. Allowance can be made for as wide price swings as the investor thinks possible; an upward "secular" (or long-term) trend can be taken into consideration, if desired; various safety devices can be used to insure against complete immobility of the plan if the

TABLE 7

VARIABLE STOCK-BOND RATIO

RESULT OF FOLLOWING SAMPLE SCHEDULE CONTROLLING STOCK SALES AND PURCHASES IN $20,000 FUND, 1937-1946

| Date | D-J Ind. average | Stock fund | % of total fund | Bond fund | % of total fund | Value of total fund |
|---|---|---|---|---|---|---|
| Jan., 1937 | 180 | $8,000 | 40% | $12,000 | 60% | $20,000 |
| *Stocks decline 16.7%* | | | | | | |
| Sept., 1937 | 150 | 6,666 | 35.7 | 12,000 | 64.3 | 18,666 |
| Increase stock fund to 50% of total | 150 | 9,333 | 50.0 | 9,333 | 50.0 | 18,666 |
| *Stocks decline 16.7%* | | | | | | |
| Nov., 1937 | 125 | 7,777 | 45.4 | 9,333 | 54.6 | 17,110 |
| Increase stock fund 60% of total | 125 | 10,266 | 60.0 | 6,844 | 40.0 | 17,110 |
| *Stocks decline 16.7%* | | | | | | |
| March, 1938 | 104⅛ | 8,555 | 55.5 | 6,844 | 44.5 | 15,399 |
| Increase stock fund to 70% of total | 104⅛ | 10,779 | 70.0 | 4,620 | 30.0 | 15,399 |
| *Stocks rise 20%* | | | | | | |
| June, 1938 | 125 | 12,935 | 73.7 | 4,620 | 26.3 | 17,555 |
| Reduce stock fund to 60% of total | 125 | 10,533 | 60.0 | 7,022 | 40.0 | 17,555 |
| *Stocks rise 20%* | | | | | | |
| Oct., 1938 | 150 | 12,640 | 64.3 | 7,022 | 35.7 | 19,662 |
| Reduce stock fund to 50% of total | 150 | 9,831 | 50.0 | 9,831 | 50.0 | 19,662 |

| Date | D-J Ind. average | Stock fund | % of total fund | Bond fund | % of total fund | Value of total fund |
|---|---|---|---|---|---|---|
| *Stocks decline 16.7%* | | | | | | |
| April, 1939 | 125 | $8,192 | 45.4 | $9,831 | 54.6 | 18,023 |
| Increase stock fund to 60% of total | 125 | 10,814 | 60.0 | 7,209 | 40.0 | 18,023 |
| *Stocks rise 20%* | | | | | | |
| Sept., 1939 | 150 | 12,977 | 64.3 | 7,209 | 35.7 | 20,186 |
| Reduce stock fund to 50% of total | 150 | 10,093 | 50.0 | 10,093 | 50.0 | 20,186 |
| *Stocks decline 16.7%* | | | | | | |
| May, 1940 | 125 | 8,410 | 45.4 | 10,093 | 54.6 | 18,503 |
| Increase stock fund to 60% of total | 125 | 11,102 | 60.0 | 7,401 | 40.0 | 18,503 |
| *Stocks decline 16.7%* | | | | | | |
| March, 1942 | 104⅛ | 9,251 | 55.5 | 7,401 | 44.5 | 16,652 |
| Increase stock fund to 70% of total | 104⅛ | 11,656 | 70.0 | 4,996 | 30.0 | 16,652 |
| *Stocks rise 20%* | | | | | | |
| Jan., 1943 | 125 | 13,987 | 73.7 | 4,996 | 26.3 | 18,983 |
| Reduce stock fund to 60% of total | 125 | 11,390 | 60.0 | 7,593 | 40.0 | 18,983 |
| *Stocks rise 20%* | | | | | | |
| July, 1944 | 150 | 13,668 | 64.3 | 7,593 | 35.7 | 21,261 |
| Reduce stock fund to 50% of total | 150 | 10,630 | 50.0 | 10,631 | 50.0 | 21,261 |
| *Stocks rise 20%* | | | | | | |
| Sept., 1945 | 180 | 12,756 | 54.5 | 10,631 | 45.5 | 23,387 |
| Reduce stock fund to 40% of total | 180 | 9,355 | 40.0 | 14,032 | 60.0 | 23,387 |
| Value, Dec. 31, 1946 | 180 | 9,355 | 40.0 | 14,032 | 60.0 | 23,387 |

market should cease to operate in the channel anticipated. But the starting point has a significance not present under the Constant Ratio and somewhat more important than under the Constant Dollar Fund.

The usual method is to decide upon a market level or area which is considered "normal" and to divide the fund between stocks and bonds in whatever proportions the investor considers most suitable for his particular purpose at that "normal" level. The schedule of decreasing stock proportions above, and increasing stock porportions below, this level is then built upon this figure, which is usually called the "median" level or zone. If the market is above or below the median when the plan is started, the investor uses as his initial ratio whatever figures are required by his plan for the then current market level.

The decision as to the median becomes vastly more important if the plan also provides that no purchases of stocks are ever to be made above the median, or sales ever made below, since under this arrangement, the plan may become immobilized if the market remains above or below the median for a long time.

In the example already given, 150 was taken as the median at which the fund was split half into bonds and half into stocks. The stock proportion was reduced ten percentage points at each 20% advance in the market, and increased ten percentage points at each 16.7% decline below it. During the 1937-1946 period 150 in the industrial average would have been a very satisfactory median point, but there is no way to be certain whether this level will prove equally satisfactory in the future.

Right here is the basic difficulty of the Variable Ratio plan. To some investors it appears a more serious problem than it does to others. Some prefer to avoid making any decision by choosing some variation of the Constant Ratio method, and being satisfied with the more moderate protection and possible profits of that type of plan.

Others have come to the conclusion that history which has repeated itself for half a century is more than likely to continue to do so. On this basis they have worked out several different means of projecting a median line or zone upon which they are willing to base a schedule and stick to it. Still others have decided that this point can be left to future judgment and combined with strict formula planning without sacrificing much of the emotional control which is the primary reason for following a formula plan.

The decision is left to the individual. The various solutions now in actual use are described in detail in Chapter XI and the arguments for and against are enumerated. The reader is urged to make up his own mind which best fits his own view of the future. From there on, once the decision has been made, the important thing is to stick to it and not let emotional thinking interfere with adherence to the plan. There has been no period yet when patience would not have paid large dividends.

# CHAPTER XI

## Methods of Selecting a Median

A variable ratio plan, as pointed out in the previous chapter, requires the selection of a "normal" or "median" market level or range. This does not mean that no value will be obtained from the plan unless an accurate choice is made; under certain variations of the plan, the significance of the median is minor, while under the others, considerable leeway exists between the highest and the lowest levels which can be expected to work reasonably well.

The better the selection of the median, however, the better the probable long-term results of the plan. This is particularly true if the plan provides that no purchases of stocks are to be made *above* the median line or zone, and no sales of stocks *below* the median. This is a simple and profitable form of delaying action which is described in greater detail further on. (Reference to the details of the Vassar Plan, given in full on pages 137-139, will help toward an understanding of the importance of median line selection.)

The first and simplest method is to study a long-term chart of some stock market index and choose by mere inspection a single level which has been crossed and re-crossed numerous times. From 1925 through 1946, for example, the area between about 120 and 150 in the Dow-Jones industrial average could be described as the median range, for about half the fluctuations were above that range and about half below. In actual practice, any level within that range would have worked reasonably well as a median line during the whole period.

Some investors have followed this method in setting up a Variable Ratio plan. One is the Sheffield Scientific School at

Yale University, which in 1944 set up just such a plan and chose 130 in the industrial average as the median line. (This is an entirely separate plan from the Yale Plan, used for the endowment of Yale University and described in Chapter IX.) No provision for changing the median is incorporated in the plan, which is of the type contemplating no purchases above or sales below the median. (See full description, pages 135-137.) Thus future functioning of the plan is dependent on either the occasional return of the average to the 130 level or future decisions of the Board of Trustees.

Not all investors are convinced that it is safe to assume that the market will continue to move above and below *any* single predetermined level. They believe that the plan itself should provide some means of keeping the median in step with the market, however imperfectly.

A long-term "moving average" of the market index used is the solution that some of these investors have chosen. They total up the figures for some number of years past (usually taking the highs and lows for each year or each month) and divide by the number of figures included to obtain the average level for the period. The result becomes the median line for one year or one month. At the end of the year or month, they cut off the first figure and add the most recent, so that at any time, the median line is the average of the market for the preceding five, ten or twenty years, as the case may be. Their belief is that if the market's typical range should change as time goes on, the new level will be reflected in the moving average in time to keep the plan working reasonably well.

Vassar College is an example of an institution which uses this means of determining the median line. The Finance Committee at different times has used both a five-year moving average and a ten-year moving average, the latter being in current use. Vassar, however, believes in using a certain amount of judgment as well as statistics and has not tied its plan irrevocably to any set method.

As a practical matter, the use of a moving average alone presents certain difficulties. Five years is a pretty short period for the smoothing out of market fluctuations (the purpose of any moving average). An unadjusted average of the preceding five years would have given a median of 215 in 1932 and 98 in 1936, neither of which would have been very satisfactory.

A ten or twenty year average does a far better job of smoothing out the fluctuations. But in a simple average of this type, the earliest year is given just as much weight in the final product as is the latest year. Investors who believe there is a secular or long-term uptrend in stock prices—as past records indicate to have been the case—fear a ten or twenty year average may be unduly low. To correct for this factor, some users of a ten year average add 15% to the figure otherwise obtained, on the theory that the growth factor is 3% a year. (The 15% figure is the result of averaging a 30% increase on the 10-year-old index, 27% on the nine-year old, etc.)

The latter method would have given a very satisfactory moving average since about 1940. Prior to that time, the abnormally high figures for 1928, 1929 and 1930 were still included in the ten-year average and the result was a higher median line than would have been completely satisfactory.

Table 8 shows the levels of the Dow-Jones industrial average which would have served as the median during each year from 1926 through 1947 on a ten-year moving average basis, both with and without the 15% increment.

With or without the adjustment, a Variable Ratio plan using a ten-year moving average as the median would, if followed strictly, have produced a satisfactory long-term investment result over the entire period since 1897. The plan for which results are portrayed in Chart 2 on page 18, is based on the use of a ten-year moving average without any adjustment for long-term growth.

From a shorter-term viewpoint, a moving average presents an additional difficulty: it may jump up or down considerably from one year to the next. This has the effect of changing the entire schedule to an extent capable, at times, of upsetting the best working of the plan. In practice, it appears desirable either to limit the amount of change in the median from one year to the next to not more than, say, five points at a time, or to place the entire plan on a monthly basis. If the moving average is recomputed each month, changes from month to month are bound to be small.

An increasing number of investors are using a "projected trend line" to determine their median line or zone. As previously

TABLE 8

TEN-YEAR MOVING AVERAGE OF DOW-JONES INDUSTRIALS

BASED ON AVERAGES OF MONTHLY MEAN PRICES AT YEAR-ENDS 1925-1946

| | Unadjusted | Increased by 15% for "secular uptrend" |
|---|---|---|
| Dec. 31, 1925 | 95 | 109 |
| Dec. 31, 1926 | 101 | 116 |
| Dec. 31, 1927 | 109 | 126 |
| Dec. 31, 1928 | 124 | 143 |
| Dec. 31, 1929 | 145 | 166 |
| Dec. 31, 1930 | 159 | 183 |
| Dec. 31, 1931 | 166 | 191 |
| Dec. 31, 1932 | 163 | 187 |
| Dec. 31, 1933 | 162 | 186 |
| Dec. 31, 1934 | 162 | 186 |
| Dec. 31, 1935 | 160 | 184 |
| Dec. 31, 1936 | 161 | 185 |
| Dec. 31, 1937 | 160 | 184 |
| Dec. 31, 1938 | 151 | 173 |
| Dec. 31, 1939 | 134 | 154 |
| Dec. 31, 1940 | 124 | 143 |
| Dec. 31, 1941 | 122 | 140 |
| Dec. 31, 1942 | 127 | 146 |
| Dec. 31, 1943 | 132 | 152 |
| Dec. 31, 1944 | 136 | 156 |
| Dec. 31, 1945 | 141 | 162 |
| Dec. 31, 1946 | 144 | 164 |

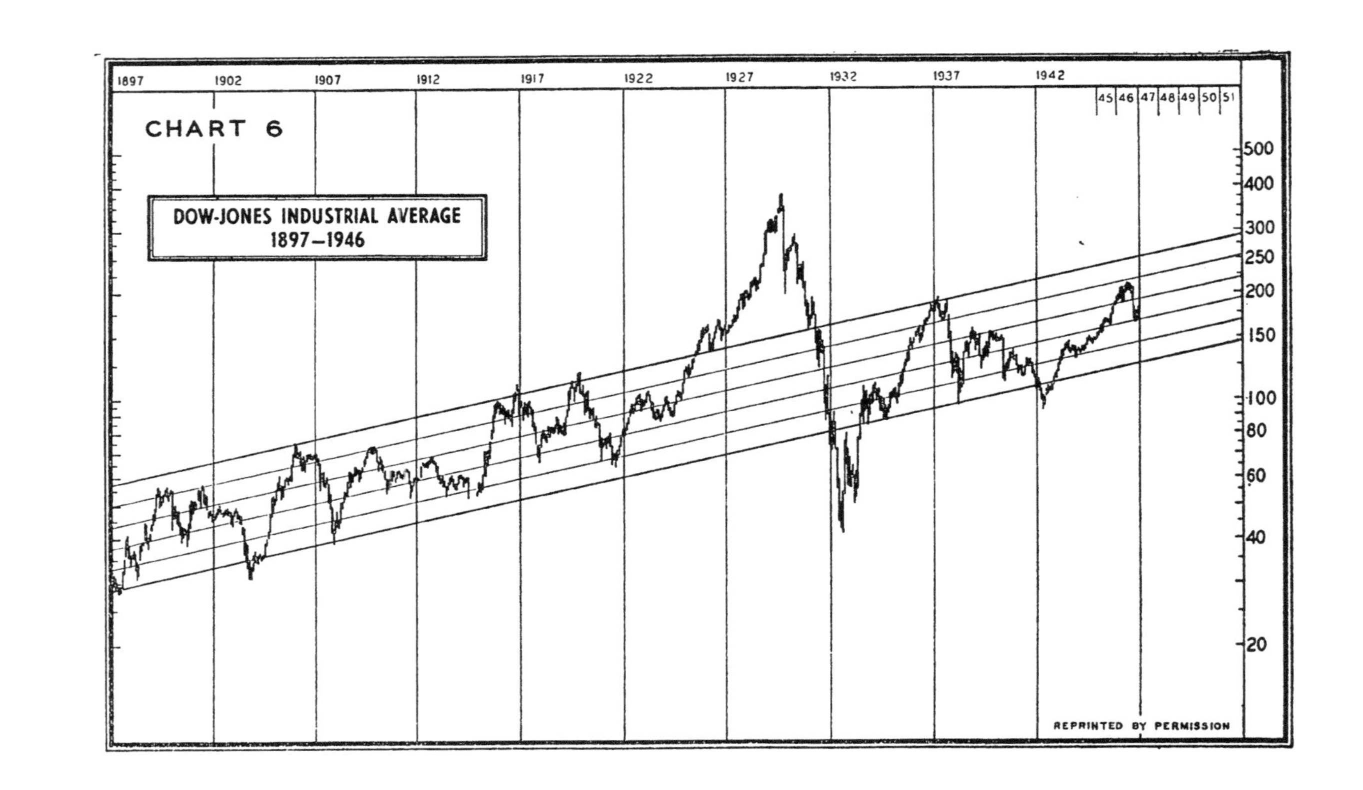
CHART 6
DOW-JONES INDUSTRIAL AVERAGE
1897—1946
1897
1902
1907
1912
1917
1922
1927
1932
1937
1942
45
46
47
48
49
50
51
500
400
300
250
200
150
100
80
60
40
20
REPRINTED BY PERMISSION

mentioned, there is a clearly defined upward trend in the Dow-Jones industrial average from the early records of 1897 through recent years. Users of the "projected trend line" assume that the rate of long-term growth which has existed in the past will continue in the future and that, therefore, a slowly rising median will provide the best results.

Back around the turn of the century, the industrial average (adjusted for an important change in the average in 1914) was fluctuating between the levels of about 30 and 55; twenty years later the comparable figures were 60 and 120, and during the period from 1935 to 1946, the lower and upper limits were about 100 and a little over 200. Investors using a "projected trend line" believe it is reasonable to expect that by 1960 the limits within which the industrial average will move will be considerably higher than in the past.

Such a trend projection is illustrated in Chart 6, which is the basis for the Seven Step Formula Plan—a widely-used plan originated by a Boston investment company organization. The upper and lower lines of the band superimposed on the industrial average from 1897 through 1946 were obtained simply by drawing straight lines through the approximate highs and lows of every major market movement with the exception of the 1929 bull and 1932 bear markets. As can be easily seen, the industrial average has broken out of this ascending channel very rarely and at the same time there have been few major market moves which did not terminate fairly close to the top or bottom of the channel.

The additional lines on the chart pertain to the working details of the Seven Step Formula Plan, which are described in a later chapter. Under this plan, the middle zone, numbered 4, is used in place of a median line. If a line were drawn through the geometric middle of that zone, however, it would provide the single median line which other forms of the Variable Ratio plan require.

To locate a single median line based on the Seven Step Plan

trend projection, connect on any chart of the industrial average (on a logarithmic scale) the point 135 at the middle of 1937 and 180 at the middle of 1947. The line can be projected into the future as far as desired and the median for any desired year read directly from the chart. Or 3% a year can simply be added to 180, which is the approximate 1947 figure.

There is some difference of opinion among investors as to whether this past long-term upward trend in stock prices can be counted upon to continue indefinitely into the future at the same rate. Some have preferred to assume a somewhat slower rate of growth from here on. They point out that the fairly steady 3% a year ascent in stock prices in the past was largely based upon the ability of corporations to plough back a good part of their earnings, instead of paying them out. They question whether corporations will be able to earn at the same rate in the future, under existing labor costs and government controls, and also whether, if earnings do continue at a comparable rate, corporations will not be forced to pay out a larger proportion of earnings in dividends to shareholders.

The formula plan of Oberlin College in effect slows up the rate of anticipated growth by using an arithmetical rather than a logarithmic chart of the Dow-Jones industrial average. A trend line was mathematically fitted from 1897 through 1926 and projected from there on to provide a median. Since it is plotted on an arithmetical scale, the rate of growth in recent years is slower than that of the Seven Step Plan. It works out to about 1½% a year during the 1940's, instead of 3% a year, and the 1947 median is 152, which compares with the Seven Step's 180.

No matter how the median is determined—simple observation, moving average, or trend projection—it is necessarily based upon either the expectation that past history will repeat itself in one way or another, or upon an outright forecast. (For a description of a plan which is based upon a long-term earnings forecast, see pages 130-132.) But many investors, realizing that considerably more profitable results can be expected from a formula plan which makes full use of a median line or zone than from other types, prefer to assume that history *will* repeat itself to a sufficient extent to make the plan work.

When all is said and done, however, just how important is the accurate selection of the median? Does success of a Variable Ratio plan depend upon the use of a median which holds close to the center of the market's fluctuations?

Mathematically, the answer is clearly that it does not. Even if the plan provides that no stock purchases are to be made when the index is above the median and no sales when it is below, the only factor of critical importance is that the median falls *within the range* of the market. (If it does not, the plan will, of course, cease to work.)

The most successful Variable Ratio plan will always be the one which comes closest to being out of stocks at the top of the market and fully invested in stocks at the bottom. In this case, the closer the median is to the center of the market's range, the better the result. But the difference in results between a plan with an accurate median and one with an extremely high or low median is less than one might expect.

For the 1937–1946 period, for example, 150 in the Dow-Jones industrials would have been close to an ideal median—it is a little above the exact geometric center, but it was reached twice (in 1938 and again in 1939) by advances which carried very little further. A plan which used 150 as a constant median and required substantial changes in the stock-bond ratio at 15% intervals above and below, would have reached a 90% stock position close to the 1938 and 1942 lows, a 35% stock position at the 1937 high and a 20% figure at the 1946 high. If the first adjustment on the way up or down was made at the median, the over-all gain in a fund using the industrial average as the stock portion and cash as the bond account would have been about 36%.

Suppose, on the other hand, that 100 had been taken as the median. The same percentage intervals and stock-bond ratios might have been used.* The maximum stock proportion would have been 50% (reached twice, in 1938 and in 1942, but maintained only until the index rose to 115) and above 152 the only adjustments would have been a reduction to a 10% stock position at each successive 15% advance. The end result would have been a gain of 28% for the ten years, compared with the 36% gain using a more ideal median. And in addition, the plan using 100 had suffered only about a 5% depreciation in capital at its lowest market value, compared with about 28% for the plan using 150.

To a considerable extent, a plan which gains an advantage in a declining period loses it when prices are rising, and vice versa. From a long-term viewpoint, keeping the median within the market's range would appear to be all that is really essential.

However, fairly accurate selection may be of importance for psychological reasons, unless the investor is above average in patience. In the example just given, the plan using 100 would have been "immobilized" at 10% stocks from October, 1938, through March, 1942, or about three and a half years. To say that this would have been difficult for any investor to endure is an obvious understatement, and the effect upon his income would have been considerable. The plan using 150, in comparison, would have required at least one transaction in every year

*The actual schedules used in this test, which were designed simply to illustrate the point and should not be considered as "recommended" for future use, were as follows:

| | Dow-Jones Industrial Average | |
|---|---|---|
| *Stock-Bond Ratio* | *150 Median* | *100 Median* |
| 10–90 | | 201 |
| 10–90 | | 174.8 |
| 10–90 | 228 | 152 |
| 20–80 | 198.4 | 132.2 |
| 35–65 | 172.5 | 115 |
| 50–50 | 150 | 100 |
| 65–35 | 130.3 | 87 |
| 80–20 | 113.2 | |
| 90–10 | 98.4 | |

The first purchase on the way down or sale on the way up was made at the median level.

except 1941 and 1943, and a total of 13 transactions during the ten years. Income would have been far more satisfactory.

The conclusion to be drawn is that every effort should be made to select a median which is and will continue to be around the center of market fluctuations, but that once the median or method of determining it is decided, the investor should stick to it. If capital safety is the prime consideration, it is better for the median to be too low than too high; if income and appreciation possibilities are the important objectives, a median that is on the high side is preferable to one that is too low.

## CHAPTER XII

### THE BASIC VARIABLE RATIO PLAN

ONCE the method of choosing a median is decided, there are several other details to be arranged in setting up a Variable Ratio plan. These are comparatively simple; it is largely a matter of choosing from a number of possible procedures those which best fit the requirements of the individual investment fund.

The more important of these details are the following:

1. The upper and lower limits of the schedule to be used.
2. The minimum and maximum stock percentages to be held if the upper and lower limits should be reached.
3. The number of steps between the upper and lower limits.
4. The "zone" or "action point" system.
5. Immediate vs. quarter-end action.
6. Other possible forms of delaying action.

So far as possible, these questions are discussed separately, but there is a certain amount of unavoidable over-lapping.

#### UPPER AND LOWER LIMITS

The range of the plan can be set in a number of ways. Upper and lower limits can be as far apart as necessary to cover any stock market action the investor believes could eventuate and it is even possible to set no such limits at all. The reason for giving the problem careful consideration is that the closer these limits come to the actual range of the market, the more effective the plan is going to be both as a protective measure and as a means of bringing about capital appreciation. The ideal Variable Ratio plan would provide for a minimum stock position at market peaks and a maximum at the lows, and the closer the plan comes to achieving this, the better the result.

Under the Seven Step Plan to which reference was made in the preceding chapter, the upper and lower limits are automatically set by the method of determining the median. The trend lines marking the upper and lower limits of the long-term channel are used as the upper and lower limits of the purchase and sale schedule. Since the channel is a rising one, the limits too become about 3% higher each year. The plan does not become completely inoperative if the stock market average rises above or falls below the channel—from there on the minimum or maximum stock percentage is maintained as if a Constant Ratio plan were being followed.

When a moving average is used to determine the median, the most convenient method of setting up a schedule is to use a certain number of percentage intervals above and below the median, since the schedule must be revised each time the median is changed.

The width of the interval and the number of intervals allowed automatically decide the upper and lower effective limits of the plan.

Among such plans now in use, the range is extremely wide. Vassar has only three selling points, at 10% intervals above the median; the median itself is the first buying point and there are three more at successive 10% intervals below. With the median at 145 (1947 figure), Vassar is entirely out of stocks above 194 and reaches its maximum stock position at 105. Oberlin College also uses a schedule based on 10% intervals, but increases and decreases its stock proportion much more gradually. The minimum ratio would only be reached above 400 in the industrial average and the maximum below 75.

A third method, which is used by the F. I. du Pont Institutional Plan in combination with a moving-average median, has no actual upper or lower limit. It, too, uses a 10% schedule.

Each time a reduction in stocks is required, the proportion of stocks is reduced by 10% of the proportion previously called for. Thus, if the stock fund is 50% at the median, it is reduced by 5%, or to 45%, at a level 10% above the median. The next reduction is 10% of 45%, or 4.5%, which brings the stock proportion to 40.5%. The process can be continued indefinitely, since each reduction is a little smaller than the preceding one. On the buying side, the same method is used.

A method which appeals to some investors—and in some respects is the simplest—is to start off by deciding how low and how high the market average appears likely to go, set those levels as the extremes, and work out the plan from there. It is important to remember, however, that the schedule should be based upon percentage intervals, rather than numbers of points. This method is illustrated later in this chapter.

### Maximum and Minimum Stock Proportions

The next detail—the smallest and the largest percentages of common stocks to be held under any circumstances—can depend entirely upon the objectives and requirements of the individual fund. Whether the range is wide or narrow will influence the results but it will not affect the operation of the plan to the extent that the choice of median or upper and lower limits may.

Institutions in general have chosen to place a relatively low maximum common stock figure—the most frequent figure is 60%. (It should be noted that Vassar College, whose plan apparently permits a 100% common stock investment, applies the plan to only half its total endowment, so than when the 100% figure is reached, only 50% of the Vassar endowment is actually invested in common stocks.) A minimum stock proportion of 20% is also a rather common figure. Vassar is an exception here, in that its plan provides for the complete elimination of common stocks.

Individual investors in many cases have gone considerably further than the usual institutional practice. Most, however, feel that a small proportion of common stocks should be held even at very high market levels as a hedge against an even further rise, and that some reserve purchasing power in the form of bonds should be maintained at correspondingly low levels. Maximums of 80% or 90% and minimums of 20% or 10% provide a degree of protection against the unexpected.

It would be incorrect to assume that a plan which goes to the extreme in either direction in this respect is necessarily more speculative or potentially more profitable than one which appears to be set up more conservatively. The width of the channel in which the plan operates has an important bearing on the situation.

So far as the minimum stock percentage is concerned, the *higher* the stock proportion carried into relatively high market levels, the greater the risk of capital depreciation in periods of declining prices. The ideal, of course, would be to have no stocks at all when a decline comes. Unfortunately, no formula plan can promise to work with precision and if this ideal is achieved, it is likely to follow a period when no stocks were held and prices were still rising.

If a minimum of 10% or 20% is used, the investor is always in a position to derive some gain from rising prices, no matter how high they may go. In addition, since the yield on stocks is usually greater than the yield on high-grade bonds, less sacrifice of current income is involved—a factor of importance to many individual investors as well as to most institutions.

Since the maximum stock proportion is reached only at historically low market levels under most plans, the risks involved in a high figure may also be less than appear. It is well to keep in mind, however, that purchases are required at various steps on the way down. Temporary immediate depreciation is bound to be encountered during any protracted decline. Many individuals can afford to wait through such a period, knowing that eventually gains will be substantial. Most institutions are understandably more reluctant to assume substantial depreciation under the same circumstances.

Usually, investors adopt a common stock figure half way between the maximum and minimum as the proportion to be held at the median line or median zone. Thus, if 20% and 60% are the minimum and maximum, then the fund is set at 40% stocks at the median. Others find it simpler to apply the plan to only part of their total fund, in such a way that a 50-50 ratio can be applied at the median, without requiring them to hold more stocks than they wish. With a $100,000 fund, for example, $40,000 might be set aside for separate bond investment and the remaining $60,000 brought under a plan which permitted 90% stock investment.

## Number of Steps

The next decision to be made is the number of buying or selling points to be provided between the upper and lower limits. Here, too, users of plans have followed widely differing patterns. The Seven Step Plan derives its name from the fact that it provides for seven such steps, which is virtually a minimum among plans in current use. The Vassar Plan also has seven buying or selling levels, covering a much narrower market range. Other institutions using Variable Ratio plans have generally provided for a greater number of steps.

The reader may recall that the long-term profit on a simple plan is the total of the profits made on each round trip between two action points. The further apart the points are, the greater the profit. Therefore, the fewer the steps, the more effective the plan, provided only that the action points are not set so far apart that important fluctuations are missed entirely. In practice, 10% or 15% intervals are in most frequent use.

With the maximum and minimum stock percentages and the number of steps between the two determined, the chief remaining decision is whether to reduce and increase the stock proportion by equal amounts at each step, or in some other way. An even division can be made: e.g., if three selling points above the median are provided and the percentage is to be decreased from

50% to 20%, the first reduction would be to 40%, the second to 30%, and the third to 20%. Some investors, however, prefer to make the first reduction (and the first increase on the buying side) a larger one, on the hypothesis that the majority of fluctuations usually occur fairly close to the median. (For an illustration, see description of Oberlin College Plan, pages 128-130)

### Example of Plan Construction

The reader must understand by now why no single formula plan can be presented as the answer to all investors' problems and why it is recommended that each of the factors described be considered in the light of individual requirements before the details of a plan are decided. The following plan is intended simply to illustrate how these considerations might be worked into a specific program, in the hope of clarifying the procedure before going on to the remaining details.

For the purpose, it is assumed that our hypothetical investor is an individual working out a Variable Ratio plan for his own use in the early part of 1947. He decides first of all that he will use a ten-year moving average of the Dow-Jones industrials, with a 15% adjustment for "secular uptrend", as his median line. He finds that the average of the monthly highs and lows from January 1, 1937, through December 31, 1946, is approximately 145 and multiplying this by 115% gives him a 1947 median of 167.

He next decides that upper and lower limits in the vicinity of 100 and 250 best fit his personal view of the probable market range for the time being. (He assumes that his moving average will rise in time to "up" his schedule if the industrial average should rise far above 250.) He wants three selling points above his median and three buying points below, and he wants them separated by equal percentage distances. He could obtain the figures he wants by using a sheet of logarithmic paper (or a slide-rule) and a ruler, and dividing the distances between 167 and 250, and 100 and 167, into three equal parts. But he decides first to see where he would come out by using 15% intervals above his median and the corresponding 13% intervals below. He finds that the figures above the median are 192; 221; and 254; while those below are 145; 126; and 110. This is close enough to the desired upper and lower limits and he decides to use them.

He wants his fund divided equally between stocks and bonds at the median, and is willing to go as heavily as 90% into stocks at his lowest purchase point. He would like to keep a minimum of 10% in stocks if his highest selling point should be reached. That gives him 40 percentage points to be disposed of, or acquired, in three steps. An equal division would give him the somewhat unwieldy figures of 13.3% increase or decrease at each step and he decides it will be simpler, and perhaps a little more profitable, to use 15% figures at each of the first two steps in either direction from the median and 10% for the third. This gives him the following schedule for the year 1947:

| Dow-Jones Industrial Average | Percentage of funds in Stocks | Percentage of funds in Bonds |
|---|---|---|
| 110 | 90% | 10% |
| 126 | 80 | 20 |
| 145 | 65 | 35 |
| Median 167 | 50 | 50 |
| 192 | 35 | 65 |
| 221 | 20 | 80 |
| 254 | 10 | 90 |

At the end of the year, he will eliminate the 1937 figures from his moving average and add those for 1947. He will then construct a new schedule in exactly the same way, based upon his 1948 median.

This is his basic plan; it covers those aspects of a Variable Ratio plan which require judgment as to the probable area of stock price fluctuations. He must also decide how he wishes to handle certain practical questions in the operation of the plan, which are discussed in the following chapter.

## CHAPTER XIII

### More About Variable Ratio Plans

At the end of the preceding chapter, a typical Variable Ratio schedule was presented. In the form given, it is based upon what is called the "action point" method of following a Variable Ratio plan, because no action is taken until the industrial average reaches the next point above or below the previous schedule point. The practical effect of this arrangement is that the percentages given for stocks and bonds apply to the area *above* the "action point" on the way up and to the area *below* it on the way down.

There is an alternative method to this, known as the "zone system." An understanding of the difference between the two will be helpful in following the remaining questions to be decided in setting up a Variable Ratio plan.

Under the "zone system," of which the Seven Step Plan is an example, levels in the industrial average are the dividing lines between zones and the percentages apply to the zones, rather than to the action points. The percentage of stocks to be held in any particular zone is thus the same whether the market is on the way up or the way down.

| | Zone | Dow-Jones Industrial Average | Percentage of fund in Stocks | Bonds |
|---|---|---|---|---|
| | 7 | 255 and over | 10% | 90% |
| | 6 | 222–254 | 20 | 80 |
| | 5 | 193–221 | 35 | 65 |
| median zone | 4 | 168–192 | 50 | 50 |
| | 3 | 146–167 | 65 | 35 |
| | 2 | 127–145 | 80 | 20 |
| | 1 | 126 and under | 90 | 10 |

A zone schedule can be illustrated by the 1947 "Investment Timetable" under the Seven Step Plan. The levels of the Dow-Jones industrial average are obtained from a long-term chart

(Chart 6 on page 88); the particular stock proportions are for a plan which contemplates a 90% maximum and 10% minimum stock position, and other figures can easily be used.

The long-term difference in results between the use of the "action point" and the "zone" methods is comparatively small if all other details are the same. There are certain differences in operation, however, which make the distinction between the two necessary at this point.

### Immediate vs. Delayed Action

When the industrial average attains a level which brings a formula plan into action, should the necessary purchase or sale be made as quickly as possible, or should all or part of the transaction be postponed? The fact that stock market trends generally continue for a period of at least several months has made it seem desirable to many formula planners to include rules for delaying action of one type or another.

Simple and usually profitable is the provision for taking action only at specified interval, such as 90 days or on a regular quarterly date. Examples given in connection with the Constant Dollar and Constant Ratio plans have demonstrated that in the majority of instances the investor will do better if he waits until such a regular date and then makes his purchase or sale (provided that the market index is still below or above, as the case may be, the significant level). Occasionally he will miss the purchase or sale, but more frequently he will obtain a considerably better price, and on a number of occasions in the past he would have benefited by an entire zone.

If he is using the "zone" method described above, he has no choice but to use a delaying action, though it does not necessarily have to be 90 days. The reason for this is that stock prices may fluctuate for a while around the point which separates two zones and if he were taking action as soon as the zone line was crossed he might have a succession of transactions too close together to do any good.

Under the "action point" method, this difficulty does not exist, and some investors prefer to take part or all of the required action as quickly as possible. For a large fund in which a certain amount of delay is unavoidable in any event, there appears to be some advantage in doing this. As a general rule for the ordinary investor, the advantage appears to be on the side of delaying transactions to the end of a quarter or some similar period.

Other forms of comparable delaying action in use by formula planners might be briefly noted:

1. Make no purchase of stocks until the average price for one month is higher than that of the preceding month; make no sale of stocks until the average price for one month is lower than that of the preceding month. (See F. I. du Pont Institutional Plan, pages 124-126).

2. Never transfer more than a fixed percentage, such as 5%, of the fund at one time, and after making such a transfer wait 60 days before making any additional purchases or sales required by the plan. (See Oberlin College Plan, pages 128-130).

3. Sell or buy only a portion of the required amount (such as one-third) immediately after the significant level is reached; permit the use of some discretion in regard to the remainder but with stop-loss provisions. (See American Board Plan, pages 121-124).

## Longer Delays

Many users of the Variable Ratio plan have incorporated into their plans a provision for never making any purchases of stocks at relatively high levels and never making any sales at relatively low levels. The usual method is simply to adopt a rule that no stock purchases will ever be made when the market index is above whatever median line or zone is used and that no stock sales will ever be made below the median. Since the median is expected to be half-way between the top and bottom of market fluctuations, such a rule has been called a "half-way rule."

A refinement of this rule is to apply it only when the index has attained a level some distance above or below the median.

The Seven Step Plan, for example, provides that if the industrial average has gone as high as Zones 6 or 7, or as low as Zones 2 or 1, no major action is subsequently taken until after the index has passed completely through Zone 4, the median zone. Otherwise, action is taken when the next zone is reached in either direction. (For example, in 1946 the market high was in Zone 5. Therefore, new purchases of stocks were made on the first quarterly date that the average fell into Zone 4.) A similar rule can be adapted by the user of a different type of Variable Ratio plan.

The effect of a half-way rule is to increase greatly the importance of the median line or zone. Without it, a Variable Ratio plan will continue to function more or less well even if the market index fails for a long period to cross the median, since profits will still be made whenever the market makes a "round trip" between any two "action points" or "zones." With the provision for never buying above and never selling below the median, it is possible for a fund to be entirely or nearly out of stocks for a long period; or, conversely, to be entirely or substantially in stocks for a long time. In either case, the potential benefit of market fluctuations above or below the median is sacrificed.

In actual practice, however, a median would have had to be very poorly chosen in the past not to have proved eventually the superiority of results from following a half-way rule. It is possible, of course, that an investor adopting such a plan in 1928 or 1929 would have selected a median so high it has never since been reached, or that in the 1932-1934 period a figure below 100 might have been selected. (Neither a trend projection or moving average method would have produced such a median, however.) Aside from these possibilities, there is no historical precedent for believing that the potentially greater profits from the use of this form of delaying action need be discarded.

The greatest benefit from such a rule is obtained when stock prices go to an extreme in either direction, such as in 1929 and 1932, 1937 and 1938, and 1942 to 1946. Purchases in a decline and sales in a rise may be postponed for a considerable time to the investor's advantage. At times when the market is fluctuating more narrowly above and below the median, it makes little difference whether the rule is followed or not.

A possibility for investors who do not wish to tie a plan so completely to the median line is to adopt the type of delaying action suggested for Constant Dollar or Constant Ratio plans. Instead of waiting for the median line to be crossed, the first purchase or sale after a change in trend might be made when a pre-determined correction of the preceding rise or decline had been accomplished. The figures of a 33.3% decline from the actual high or a 50% advance from the actual low might be used to determine the levels at which the original schedule once again took effect, if these levels were reached before the market index returned to the median.

This method would not insure profits from the smaller market movements which are counter to the major market trend and which are the chief advantage of using no delaying action of this type at all. Its advantage over the straight use of the median line is only that it might take care of the formula planner's problem if the market should move permanently into a different price range from that anticipated when the plan was designed.

### Transfers within the Zone

It has been assumed so far that the investor does nothing between the times when the market index moves from one significant point or zone to another. This is the practice followed by many formula plan investors, and under many plans it is the only practicable procedure.

However, the investor who makes his adjustments only on regular quarterly dates (or at some other regular interval) has a choice in this respect. He can, if he wishes, maintain the required percentage of the zone or of the most recent action point, by making the necessary small purchase or sale on his regular date for valuing his fund. For example, assume that on January 1 of a hypothetical year, an investor was using 150 as his median and the market index had risen from a lower level to 152. His schedule calls for an equal balance between stocks and bonds at this point and he makes it. The next sale of stocks called for by his schedule will be at 172 in the index.

At the end of March, the index stands at 167, or five points short of his next selling level. A valuation of his fund shows him that his stocks are no longer 50% of the total, but 52½%. At this point he would sell enough stocks to bring the proportion down to 50% again.

If stock prices continue to rise, he will have reduced his profit very slightly by selling a minor amount of stocks earlier than if he had waited for the 172 level. On the other hand, if the 172 level is never reached, he has taken a small amount of money out of stocks and he is just that much better off when prices go down. Investors who use this method maintain the required percentages even if it means buying stocks above the median or selling them below. Thus, if our hypothetical investor found at the end of June that the market index was back to 152 and therefore still above his median, he would nevertheless buy back enough stocks to bring his percentage back to 50. He would have a small profit to show for the successive sale and re-purchase.

From the viewpoint of long-term capital appreciation, it does not appear to make much difference whether transfers of this nature within the zone are made or not. Other considerations, however, may make it a desirable addition to many plans. For one thing, it establishes the habit of valuing the fund at a regular interval and with the expectation that some action will be taken. The investor who has acquired this habit is not likely either to overlook the necessary action when an important change should be made or to shy away from making it.

In the second place, the formula plans which, because of the delaying actions provided, are most successful in the long run, are almost certain to encounter periods as long as several years when no action at all is called for. It is natural to become impatient and the psychological advantage of a plan which calls for *some* action at regular intervals should therefore not be underestimated.

If the fund is relatively small, some of the transfers required under this method may be too minor to bother with. The investor can set either a minimum dollar figure or a minimum percentage of his fund, such as 2%, and do nothing on the dates when the required change would be less than this.

## CHAPTER XIV

### Results of Variable Ratio Plans

Earliest actual user of a Variable Stock-Bond Ratio plan known to the author is Vassar College, whose plan was adopted in June, 1938. Practical experience in plan operation covering eight and one-half years is therefore available and provides the logical starting point for an examination of the actual and potential results of the Variable Ratio type of plan.

Fortunately, Vassar kept a record for this period of just what happened to the original $3,000,000 fund which commenced operating under the plan on June 30, 1938. No new money was added to it and when, in 1940, it was decided to bring an additional part of the endowment under the plan, a separate fund was set up. Also, Vassar's common stock investments have been restricted to investment-type issues whose fluctuations are similar to those of the Dow-Jones industrial average. The results, as compared with the market index, can be primarily attributed to the plan rather than to superior security selection.

The value of Vassar's "Stock Fund No. 1" on various dates between the plan's adoption and the end of 1946, with changes in value compared with the Dow-Jones industrial average, was as follows:

| Date | Dow-Jones Industrial Average | Total Value Vassar Fund | %Increase or Decrease from June 30, 1938 | % Change in D-J Av. from June 30, 1938 |
|---|---|---|---|---|
| June 30, 1938 | 133.88 | $3,000,000 | .... | .... |
| June 30, 1941 | 123.14 | 3,185,130 | 6.2% | -8.0% |
| June 30, 1942 | 103.34 | 2,716,030 | -9.0 | -22.8 |
| Dec. 31, 1943 | 135.89 | 3,710,758 | 23.7 | 1.5 |
| Dec. 31, 1945 | 192.91 | 4,151,148 | 38.4 | 44.1 |
| Dec. 31, 1946 | 177.20 | 4,144,484 | 38.15 | 32.4 |

Working details of the Vassar Plan are given on pages 137-139 and comments in regard to the general method followed have been included in the preceding chapters. It should be noted that the plan has been followed strictly; the one detail in which current judgment is permitted is the annual selection of the median line, which is principally determined from a moving average, but not without additional consideration from the Finance Committee.

As previously pointed out, the fund to which the Vassar plan applies is only part of the total endowment. It was accordingly permitted to go entirely into common stocks in 1942 when the industrial average fell to the third buying point, a little under 100. Sales of stocks were begun in late 1943 and made in successive stages on the way up until late 1945, when the final sales of stocks were made at an average level of 180. From that time through the end of 1946 no stocks were held.

Vassar's results illustrate a number of interesting points. Most obvious, of course, is the fact that the best results, as compared with the industrial stock average, were achieved in the first five years of plan operation, when the market was fluctuating in a comparatively narrow range. At the end of 1943, the gain of 23.7% in the Vassar fund compared with a 1.5% increase in the industrial average.

From that time on, the successive reductions in common stocks while the market was rising resulted in a less favorable comparison. At the end of 1945, the fund had increased less than the average for the entire period since 1938. But by the end of 1946, when the average was still 32% above the starting level, the Vassar fund was appreciably better off than if it had been entirely invested in common stocks throughout the eight and a half years and it was in a strong defensive position.

Hypothetical results for other Variable Ratio plans over the same period and over much longer periods in the past in most cases indicate the possibility of greater capital appreciation than the Vassar Plan has achieved. The distinction between actual results of a plan in operation at the time and past hypothetical results of a plan designed more recently, is largely a question of how much hindsight has entered into the formulation of the recent plan. To eliminate hindsight is more difficult with a Variable Ratio plan than with the Constant Dollar or Constant Ratio types.

So far as the choice of median is concerned, a moving average method comes close to eliminating hindsight, if one method is followed consistently. The projected trend method is in a somewhat different category, since the trend that determines the median is itself the past record of the market. However, both of the projected trends described in this book (the Oberlin and the Seven Step) could have been obtained in much their present form by the early 1920's. It is fair to say that the hypothetical experiences of plans using this method over the past 25 years are reasonable representations of what could have been accomplished in actual practice.

The hypothetical results which follow are of two types, each included for a different purpose. Most valuable for judging the potentialities of Variable Ratio plans are the long-term and 1937–1946 results of the du Pont Institutional Plan and the Seven Step Plan, representing the use of the moving average and trend projection methods, respectively. The former plan has been applied to the Dow-Jones industrial average for the entire 50 years from 1897 to the end of 1946, the latter for the 25 years from 1922 to the end of 1946.

A second set of hypothetical results is based on a simple Variable Ratio plan, using a fixed 150 median, for the 1937–1946 period. Results for the volatility and management indexes are shown on the basis of this plan. It very obviously entails the use of hindsight since, as previously noted, 150 would have been an advantageous median to use during that period. Neither the use of a fixed median nor the selection of the 150 level is recommended—it is simply the most convenient method for computing a number of results. The only purpose of the hypothetical examples based upon the particular plan is to illustrate the effects of volatility on this type of plan. In other words, the results of using it can be compared with each other, but that is as far as they are intended to be used.

The long-term result of the du Pont Institutional Plan has already been shown graphically in Chart 2 (page 18); the details of the plan will be found on pages 124-126. A million dollar fund started in April, 1895, would have grown to nearly seven and a half million dollars by the end of 1946. From the 1929 high value to the 1932 low, the fund would have declined approximately 55%, but it would have been back to the 1929 high value by May, 1935. By the 1937 high, it would have been worth over 60% more than in 1929, and from the 1937 high to the 1946 high, it had grown an additional 17%.

The results from the start of 1937 to the end of 1946 can be translated into terms of a $20,000 fund, for comparison with other plans. Since the calculations are based upon monthly mean prices for the industrial average, rather than daily closing prices as in the other examples, it is necessary to start this hypothetical example in October, 1936, in order to have the starting and closing levels of the market approximately equal.

F. I. du PONT INSTITUTIONAL PLAN

| Date | Dow-Jones ind. avge. | Market Value of Fund |
|---|---|---|
| October, 1936 | 172.94 | $20,000 |
| April, 1938 | 112.01 | 16,900 |
| November, 1938 | 152.28 | 20,720 |
| April, 1942 | 97.71 | 16,860 |
| June, 1946 | 205.73 | 24,920 |
| December, 1946 | 172.39 | 23,560 |

A second Variable Ratio plan which can satisfactorily be worked back a considerable number of years is the Seven Step Plan, which is based upon a trend projection. (See comments in preceding chapters and pages 132-135 for complete description.) There is no question that much the same broad channel now in use could have been drawn by 1921. If on January 1, 1922, a $1,000,000 fund had started to operate according to the Seven

Step Plan, using the Dow-Jones industrials as the aggressive portion and cash for the defensive side, by December 31, 1946, the fund would have grown to more than $3,700,000. The hypothetical results for the entire 25-year period are illustrated in Chart 7.

CHART 7

HYPOTHETICAL SEVEN STEP PLAN FUND 1922–1946

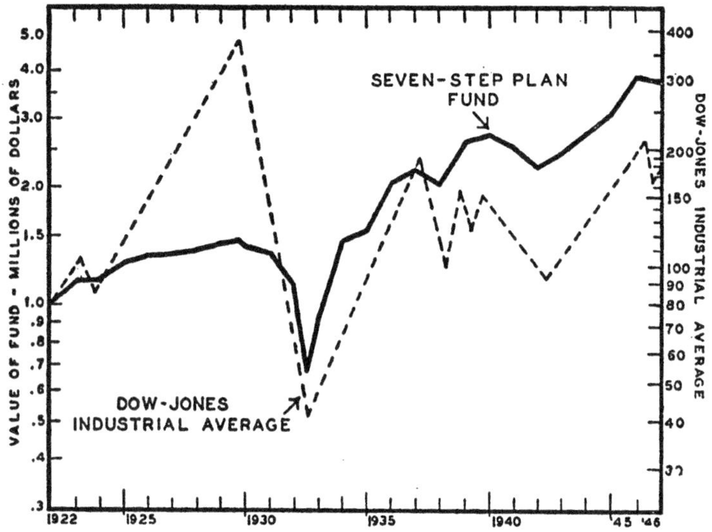

For the 1937–1946 period alone, capital growth under the Seven Step Plan for a fund using the industrial average as the stock portion would have been about 70%. The following results are at the closing market levels on the dates shown:

SEVEN STEP FORMULA PLAN

| Date | Dow-Jones ind. avge. | Market Value of Fund |
|---|---|---|
| January 1, 1937 | 180 | $20,000 |
| March 31, 1938 | 98.95 | 16,392 |
| December 31, 1938 | 154.76 | 23,626 |
| March 31, 1942 | 99.53 | 18,915 |
| June 30, 1946 | 205.62 | 35,186 |
| December 31, 1946 | 180 | 33,927 |

The results of these two plans, which in a general way represent the moving average and projected trend methods of median selection, are not truly comparable, for a number of reasons. If they are compared with each other, the following points should be taken into consideration:

1. The moving average method virtually guarantees that the market index must sooner or later return to the median, since the index itself determines the median. Any trend projection method depends upon the belief that past history will repeat itself. That it has done so rather consistently up to the date of publication is the primary basis for accepting it.

2. The two particular plans used for examples differ widely in the range of market fluctuation for which provision is made. The Seven Step Plan uses minimum and maximum stock percentages of 10% and 90%. The minimum and maximum reached by the du Pont Plan were actually 10.2% and 96.4% (in 1929 and 1932 respectively), but much wider fluctuations are required to reach these extremes. Under the Seven Step Plan, the minimum stock figure is reached at a level approximately 100% above that at which the maximum applies. The du Pont Plan has no actual minimum stock percentage, but from a 90% stock position to 10% requires about a 300% rise in the market index.

For practical purposes, it might be said that the du Pont Plan, or any similarly constructed plan, is designed to fit as well as possible any conceivable future trend in common stock prices. The Seven Step Plan, or any trend projection method which is designed to secure maximum capital growth from moderate fluctuations above and below the median, will prove more satisfactory so long as the market index fluctuates in the general neighborhood of the expected channel.

Just as with other types of formula plans, results derived from a Variable Ratio Plan depend to a highly important extent upon the volatility of the securities used for the stock portion. For the 1937–1946 period, Low-Priced stocks produced more than three times the capital growth that the use of the industrial average did, Highly Speculative stocks more than four times.

The hypothetical results, based on the same indexes previously used for other types of plans, are shown in Table 9. As already stated, the plan used for this purpose makes no pretense of being either scientific or free from the use of hindsight, though it might be noted that the result, when it is applied to the industrial average, is less impressive than that provided by use of the Seven Step Plan. A fixed median of 150 was used and the "half-way rule" was applied. The complete schedule followed was:

| Dow-Jones ind. avge. | Proportion of fund in Stocks | Bonds |
|---|---|---|
| 98.4 | 90% | 10% |
| 113.2 | 80 | 20 |
| 130.3 | 65 | 35 |
| 150 | 50 | 50 |
| 172.5 | 35 | 65 |
| 198.4 | 20 | 80 |
| 228.2 | 10 | 90 |

Adjustments in the funds were made only at the ends of calendar quarters.

Income estimates for the Variable Ratio plan were also made on the basis of the simple plan used to show the effects of volatility. On a $20,000 fund which used the industrial average for the stock portion and obtained a 2% average rate on the bond portion, total income for the ten years would have been $8,864 under this plan. The figure compares with income of $7,551 if the entire $20,000 had been placed in stocks at the start and no changes made, or $5,776 if $10,000 had been placed in stocks and $10,000 in bonds at 2%, and no changes made. Income was higher under the plan than on a complete stock investment in every year of the ten with the exceptions of 1937 and 1946, the two years when the stock position, because of high prices, was lowest.

TABLE 9

VARIABLE STOCK-BOND RATIO

RESULTS OF USING SAMPLE PLAN IN $20,000 FUND 1937–1946 WITH VARIOUS TYPES OF SECURITIES AS STOCK PORTION

| Class of Security | Value of fund Dec. 31, 1946 | Lowest value during 10 yrs |
|---|---|---|
| Dow-Jones industrial average | $30,670 | $15,603 |
| Business Cycle Stocks | 38,358 | 14,447 |
| Low-Priced Stocks | 56,330 | 12,596 |
| Highly Speculative Stocks | 65,484 | 12,742 |
| Fully Managed Stock Fund | 42,019 | 15,182 |
| Fully Managed Stock Fund without use of plan | | |
| (a) $10,000 in stocks, $10,000 in bonds | $23,150 | $15,020 |
| (b) $20,000 in stocks | 26,300 | 10,040 |

However, it would not be safe to conclude that a Variable Ratio plan will consistently produce higher income than a complete common stock investment. Especially if the "half-way rule" for making no stock purchases above the median is included in the plan, the investor who is dependent upon current income from investments needs to consider the potential effect of reductions in common stock holdings which might continue in effect for a protracted period.

This is a problem which colleges and similar institutions in particular have faced. They do not want to reduce the quality of their bond holdings, in the search for income, to a point where important risks are involved; at the same time, a reasonably steady in come is necessary.

Two solutions have been found. One is to plan for a fairly large minimum stock position even at high prices—20% is a frequently-used figure. The second is to set up an income reserve out of income in the good years, or even, in a few cases, from the realized profits which are attributed to the use of the plan.

## Postscript—September, 1947

In the course of many discussions with interested investors, the remark was several times heard that 1947 might be a crucial year for formula planning. The background of this statement was the fact that a full year after the 1946 bull market high, the industrial average had not declined sufficiently to bring a good many plans into action on the buying side. Sales of stocks had been made successfully on the way up, but many plans called for no purchases above the 145–150 level.

This was true of Constant Dollar or Constant Ratio plans which provided for no purchases until a 33⅓% decline from peak prices had been reached, and of many Variable Ratio plans where a half-way rule was in effect. Of the plans of that type described in this book, only the Seven Step Plan had reached a buying level.

By the time this book can be published the question may have resolved itself through a further decline sufficient to bring the plans into operation. But it is equally possible that a new major advance will have taken place. In such a case the reader will be able to see clearly that many formula plans "missed the boat" by not requiring purchases around the low levels of 1946 and early 1947.

If one holds strictly to the postulate that a formula plan must be completely automatic, then such an occurrence would have to be accepted as an unfortunate "break" similar to a number which have taken place in the past, distressing at the time but of little importance when the final score is totalled up.

In the event that common stock prices rise above their 1946 highs without first going lower than they had by the spring of 1947, it is a safe guess that stock market technicians will argue for years whether or not the 1946-1947 decline was properly classified as a major bear market. Certainly on a long-term chart it will look like no more than an important secondary reaction, comparable to that of 1934 or to a number of intermediate advances during past bear markets.

It is not the purpose of most formula plans to "catch" the smaller stock price fluctuations. The position of the "orthodox" formula planner in September, 1947, if his plan had not required stock purchases, was that he would make additional sales of stock at higher levels, if they were reached, but that from a long-term viewpoint the exercise of patience in buying common stocks was more likely than not to be rewarded.

In actual practice, however, a number of formula planners have replaced at least part of the stocks they sold at higher levels on the way up. The reasons given by one of these for taking action before the plan required it are included in Chapter IV, together with a general rule which can be followed by any investor who runs into serious doubts as to whether he should abide strictly by his plan at all times.

To repeat, the vitally important aspect of following a plan is to take the required action with automatic precision when the plan says "buy stocks" or "sell stocks". The only safe method to follow if it is desired to postpone the purchase or sale is to place standing "stop-loss" orders at the required level.

The situation is somewhat different when the deviation from the plan consists of taking action in either direction *before* the plan requires it. Provided that stocks can be replaced at lower levels than they were sold, or sold above the prices at which the corresponding purchases took place, the investor will still have retained at least part of the capital growth resulting from the use of the plan.

To be specific, take the case of an investor who had sold $10,000 worth of stocks at 155, at 178 and at 205 when these levels were reached in 1945 and 1946. (The average price he would have realized would have been just under 180). In late

1946 and early 1947 he would have had $30,000 in cash as the result of those sales. His plan, perhaps, does not require any stock purchases above 150. But he is impatient after waiting a full year, he sees that dividend yields on stocks are considerably higher than he can obtain on good-grade bonds and he would like the additional income, and he is willing to take a small gamble on the chance that the decline is only an interruption of the bull market. Perhaps of greater importance, he also sees that while the industrial average, at 170, is only 17% below the level at which he made his final sale, the prices of the particular stocks he sold are 40% below the prices he obtained.

If he invests at that point only the $10,000 he took out of stocks at 205, he knows that whatever happens he has already saved himself $4,000 by following the plan. If stock prices fall a lot lower, it is true he will have a loss on that $10,000 he would have avoided by waiting until the plan called for the purchase. But if he had had no plan and had remained fully invested in stocks the whole time, his position in respect to that particular block of his capital would be little different, except that instead of having $10,000 of stocks he would have only $6,000. If prices go up, he will be considerably better off.

This example is not given as a recommended procedure but only to illustrate the one way in which a plan can be made flexible without incurring the risk of losing the gains the use of a plan has produced. It is the type of question an individual can best decide for himself in the light of the particular circumstances which may exist if he should face a similar situation in the future. The investor who prefers to eliminate any such attempt at combining judgment with a purely automatic plan has on his side the weight of evidence that in the majority of past instances the best results would have been obtained by the patient investor.

# PART III

# FORMULA PLANS IN CURRENT USE

In this section have been brought together the details of nine specific plans which are currently being used by investors. In these descriptions will be found both the answers to certain practical details of operation under a formula plan and a number of interesting provisions which could not conveniently be worked into the general description in the preceding section.

The plans chosen for full description by no means represent all of the formula plans known to be in operation. The choice was made primarily in order to provide as wide a variety of approaches to the subject as possible, and was also dictated in part by the willingness of planners to make public the details of their methods. The author is extremely grateful to the organizations represented for their permission to publish the specifications of their investment plans.

They have been arranged in alphabetical order.

## A VARIABLE RATIO PLAN WITHOUT A MEDIAN LINE

FUND TO WHICH APPLIED: American Board of Commissioners for Foreign Missions.

DATE PLAN ADOPTED: September, 1942 (subsequently revised).

APPROXIMATE SIZE OF FUND: Total fund of about $9,000,000 is divided into a Bond Fund and an Equity Fund, which are kept approximately equal in amount. The plan applies only to the Equity Fund, which is itself ordinarily divided between stocks and bonds.

GENERAL TYPE OF PLAN: Variable stock-bond ratio, based upon level of Dow-Jones industrial average. Upper and lower possible expected limits are set, but no choice of median in the ordinary sense is required and either purchases or sales may take place in any part of the determined range. Method of determining amount of stocks to be bought or sold, and inclusion of a permissive form of delaying action, are designed to increase potential gains over the profits normally expected from this type of variable ratio plan.

WORKING DETAILS:

1. Shifts from stocks to bonds, and vice versa, are made whenever the Dow-Jones industrial average reaches any of the following points, which are set at 15% intervals: 75, 87, 100, 115, 132, 152, 175, 201, 231, 265, 305, 351, 404.

2. Purchases of stocks made at the above levels in a declining market are made in constant dollar amounts; i.e., $300,000 has been set as the amount to be released for stock purchases each time a decline carries across the next lower level of the scale. This automatically increases the proportion of the fund in stocks as the market declines.

Under this plan, it is necessary to have in the "reserve" or "bond" portion of the fund, sufficient money for successive purchases downward to "the lowest reasonable level which the Committee foresees." Above 152, for example, if it is desired to be able to make purchases as low as 75, it is necessary to have six times $300,000, or $1,800,000 in the reserve portion.

3. Sales of stocks are made in variable amounts, depending on the level of the market. The amount released for transfer to the Reserve at each level is equal to the industrial average multiplied by $2,000. At 100, therefore, the figure would be $200,000; at 150 it would be $300,000, or the same as the purchase figure; at 200 it would be $400,000. The proportion of stocks is thus automatically reduced as the market rises. Under this method, the fund is completely out of stocks when a high enough level is reached so that the required sale is greater than the amount of stocks then in the fund. What the level will be depends upon the amount of the stock fund at the start: under the American Board plan, a sale at 404 would complete the liquidation of stocks.

A special provision is necessary to take care of "jiggles" in the market—that is, when a long up or down trend is interrupted by a move in the opposite direction sufficient to bring the plan into action. If, for example, the market is rising and a sale is called for at 231, $462,000 of stocks would be sold. Suppose it then declined to 201, the next lower purchase point. Only $300,000 would be re-invested. If the market then rose again to 231, that $300,000 would be worth only $345,000, so that if the usual rule were followed and $462,000 of stocks again sold, too much would have been taken out of stocks at the same market level. So in this case, sales would be limited to the $345,000 figure.

The same rule is applied, in reverse, when purchases are being made in a declining market and the customary $300,000 standard purchase figure is greater than the amount of stocks previously sold.

4. *Delaying Provisions*—On sales only 20% of the total amount is sold automatically as soon as the sales level is

reached; on purchases, the corresponding figure is $33\frac{1}{3}\%$. On the remainder, the Committee has a certain amount of discretion, which permits postponing sales or purchases of stocks which would otherwise be made too early in an extended rise or decline.

The wording of the American Board plan in regard to sales is:

a. The first block (20%) will be sold promptly after the sales level is reached.

b. The second block (40%) will be sold whenever the Dow-Jones industrial average declines 2% from a previous high, using closing prices for measurement.

c. The third block (40%) may be sold above the highest release level reached at any time in whole or in part at the discretion of the Treasurer and two members of the Finance Committee; and in any event will be sold either upon a 2% decline which carries the Dow-Jones industrial average below the last release level or upon a decline to the last release level if such decline is greater than 2%.

The procedure in the case of purchases is:

a. The first block ($\frac{1}{3}$) will be invested promptly after the purchase level is reached.

b. The second block ($\frac{2}{3}$) may be invested below the lowest release level reached at any time in whole or in part at the discretion of the Treasurer and two members of the Finance Committee. In the exercise of this discretion serious consideration will be given to investment of any uninvested portion of this block, either upon a 2% rise which carries the Dow-Jones industrial average above the last purchase level or upon a rise to the last purchase level if such rise is greater than 2%.

5. *Securities Used*—The reserve portion consists mainly

of highest grade bonds, but a limited proportion of preferred stocks of investment quality may be held at times in order not to "penalize the income account too severely."

Investment-type common stocks comprise the equity portion.

Because of the nature of the plan, the question of whether bonds are carried at market or book value is unimportant.

REMARKS:

Experience under this plan is somewhat limited, since it was started only in 1942 and has been revised since that time. Its primary advantages appear to lie in the avoidance of the median line problem and the ability to capitalize on the more substantial intermediate fluctuations. It does not, however, obviate the need for setting upper and lower limits within which the plan will operate.

## F. I. DU PONT INSTITUTIONAL PLAN

FUND TO WHICH APPLIED: A sample plan provided by New York Stock Exchange firm of Francis I. du Pont & Company, 1 Wall Street, New York, N. Y., for use of institutional investors.

GENERAL TYPE OF PLAN: Variable stock-bond ratio, based upon ten-year moving average of Dow-Jones industrial average. For long-term hypothetical results, see Chart 2, page 18.

WORKING DETAILS:

1. *Median Line*—Determined monthly by averaging the monthly mean prices of the Dow-Jones industrials for the preceding ten years. No purchases ever are made when the actual monthly mean price of the Dow-Jones industrials is above its 10-year average; no sales ever are made when the actual monthly mean price is below the 10-year average. Whenever the actual monthly mean price advances or declines to the 10-year average, the proportion of funds invested in

common stocks is reduced or increased to 50% of the total market value of the fund.

The decision to use a 10-year moving average is explained as follows: "We decided to use a 10-year average simply because we believe that 10 years constitute a long enough period to include some good and bad times in any past or probable future segment of American life . . . . . . Unless prices should advance at an ever increasing pace to infinity, or decline at a constantly increasing rate to zero, they inevitably would return from time to time to their average, because they determine the average. Recognizing the fact that actual prices determine the average, we find it possible to accept the average as 'normal' without thereby implying any opinion as to the future course of stock prices."

2. *Buying and Selling Schedule*—Sales are made above the median on a 10% schedule which is so designed that the proportion of stocks in the fund is constantly decreased but would never reach 0, regardless of how high the market average rose. When the monthly mean price of the industrial average reaches 110% of its 10-year average, the schedule calls for a reduction in common stocks by 10% of 50%, or by 5% to 45%. When the monthly mean price reaches 120% of its 10-year average, the schedule calls for a reduction in common stocks by 10% of 45%, or by 4.5% to 40.5%. This process can be continued indefinitely, each reduction in common stocks being 10% of the proportion previously called for by the plan.

Purchases are made below the median on a similar schedule. A "percentage equivalents" scale is set, which results in required purchases at 90.9%, 83.3%, 76.9%, 71.4%, 66.6% etc. of the 10-year average. At each increase the proportion of funds invested in common stocks is increased on a schedule corresponding to that for sales on the way up.

3. *Delaying Provisions*—The "half-way rule" is applied, in that no purchases are ever made above the median, or sales

below. In addition, no purchases of common stocks called for by the index are made until the actual monthly mean price of the Dow-Jones industrial average advances for one month above the mean price for the month before; no sales of common stocks called for by the index are made until the actual monthly mean price of the Dow-Jones industrial average declines for one month below the mean price for the month before.

This rule is based upon past statistical records showing that if stock prices have risen in a given month, there is better than a 50–50 chance that they will also rise in the following month. If stock prices have declined, they are more likely to decline than to rise in the following month. On a few occasions the rule has resulted in purchases or sales at less favorable levels than if they had been made immediately, but over any long period of time this form of delaying action has added considerably to the results produced by the plan.

## KENYON COLLEGE PLAN

FUND TO WHICH APPLIED: Endowment Fund of Kenyon College, Gambier, Ohio.

DATE PLAN ADOPTED: March, 1941.
APPROXIMATE SIZE OF FUND: Slightly under $2,000,000.
GENERAL TYPE OF PLAN: Constant Ratio.

WORKING DETAILS:

*Normal Ratio:* Cash and Fixed Yield Securities 60%; Equities 40%.

*Provision for maintaining ratio*: "When by market fluctuations, the percentage of equities shall increase above 40% of the total, no additional common stocks will be purchased. When the percentage of equities shall decrease below 40% of the total, common stocks will not be further reduced by sales.

"At such extended intervals as the Committee may determine but presumably not oftener than annually, securities shall be sold or purchased as necessary to adjust the portfolio to the original specified percentages. It is not anticipated that these points of adjustment will coincide with the tops and bottoms of a fluctuating stock market, but that such adjustments, repeated as necessary, will automatically reduce stock holdings at higher levels and increase stocks at lower levels and over the long term obtain a common stock portfolio at costs not in excess of their permanent long term value."

In practice, the adjustments have been made when the stock-bond ratio was from three to six percentage points away from the "normal" ratio.

*Securities Used*—Of the total fund, 10% is retained in cash, short term bonds and government bonds of fixed redeemable value, to facilitate the operation of the plan. 50% of the fund is invested in other bonds and preferred stocks of investment grade. Preferred stocks "of lesser quality" are classed with equities. Diversification is maintained by using as a normal unit of investment $25,000 in the bonds of any one corporation and $10,000 in the stock of any one corporation. Securities are carried at market value.

REMARKS:

This is an example of a plan in which a certain amount of judgment plays a part, since no rule is fixed for conditions under which purchases or sales of stocks must be made. In six years of operation, however, the results obtained have indicated that this limited amount of judgment can be satisfactorily combined with a formula operation. Stocks were purchased in May, 1942 (around 95); sold in June, 1943 (142); in late 1945 and early 1946 (181–212); and purchased in October, 1946 (172).

The over-all increase in value of the Kenyon fund from March 1, 1941, to February 1, 1947, was nearly 30%, compared with about 19% if the fund had been placed 40% in the Dow-Jones industrial average and 60% in cash and no changes made.

In addition, the following conclusions have been drawn by the Kenyon Investment Committee:

1. Operation of the Kenyon Plan has prevented any major mistakes in the direction and timing of equity transactions.
2. Limitation on the selection of new equity purchases to the adverse environment of relatively deflated markets and the necessity of sales of the weakest stocks at higher levels has served to improve the average quality and yield.
3. The cumulative gain over average market performance has provided a margin of safety in conservation of capital.
4. The Kenyon Plan has greatly facilitated the work of the Investment Committee. Having agreed on major principles, the Committee has experienced no difficulty in acting promptly and unanimously on all individual transactions over a six-year period.

## GUIDANCE PLAN OF OBERLIN COLLEGE

FUND TO WHICH APPLIED: Endowment of Oberlin College, Oberlin, Ohio.

DATE PLAN ADOPTED: In use as a guide for control of equity holdings since 1944.

APPROXIMATE SIZE OF FUND: Over $25,000,000.

GENERAL TYPE OF PLAN: Variable stock-bond ratio based upon level of Dow-Jones industrial average. Provides for a progressive median line based upon secular trend. Strict adherence to plan would prevent stock purchases above median line or sales below it, but in practice Investment Committee has used plan as a guide rather than an inviolable rule.

WORKING DETAILS:

1. *Median Line*—Based upon secular trend mathematically established for the years 1897 through 1925 and projected on an arithmetical scale into the future indefinitely. Trend line can be approximately located on any arithmetical chart of Dow-Jones industrials by drawing a straight line through 121 at the end of 1933 and 152 at the end of 1947, and projecting as far as desired in either direction. Annual rate of rise in median is about $1\frac{1}{2}$%.

2. *Purchase and Sale Schedule*—Plan applies to entire endowment. A 40% stock—60% bond position is considered "normal" and applies at the median level. The stock percentage is reduced at each 10% rise above the median and reduced at each 10% fall below the median. A maximum stock position of 65% and a minimum of 10% are planned, but would be reached only above 400 or below 75 in the Dow-Jones industrials. Larger percentage acquisitions or disposals are provided within the relatively narrow ranges above and below the median, with smaller changes as the extremes are reached.

The schedules in effect during 1947 and 1948 are as follows:

| | % in Common Stocks | Level of Dow-Jones Ind. Average 1947 | 1948 |
|---|---|---|---|
| 11th 10% Rise | 10 | 433 | 440 |
| 10th 10% Rise | 12 | 394 | 400 |
| 9th 10% Rise | 14 | 358 | 364 |
| 8th 10% Rise | 16 | 325 | 331 |
| 7th 10% Rise | 18 | 295 | 301 |
| 6th 10% Rise | 20 | 268 | 274 |
| 5th 10% Rise | 23 | 244 | 249 |
| 4th 10% Rise | 26 | 222 | 226 |
| 3rd 10% Rise | 29 | 202 | 205 |
| 2nd 10% Rise | 32 | 184 | 186 |
| 1st 10% Rise | 35 | 167 | 169 |
| Median | 40 | 152 | 154 |
| 1st 10% Fall | 45 | 137 | 139 |
| 2nd 10% Fall | 50 | 123 | 125 |
| 3rd 10% Fall | 53 | 111 | 112 |
| 4th 10% Fall | 56 | 100 | 101 |
| 5th 10% Fall | 59 | 90 | 91 |
| 6th 10% Fall | 62 | 81 | 82 |
| 7th 10% Fall | 65 | 73 | 74 |

If the average should go higher or lower than this schedule contemplates, the 10% or 65% stock percentage would be re-established at each additional 10% advance or decline.

3. *Delaying Actions*—No purchases or sales are made at less than 60-day intervals, and at no time is more than 5% of the account bought or sold at once. Thus, if the transfer of more than 5% of the total fund from bonds to stocks is required, only 5% can be moved at once and 60 days must elapse before the remainder is transferred.

4. *Securities Used and Method of Valuation*—All general investments, including mortgages and real estate which are included with bonds for purposes of the plan, come under the guidance plan. Securities are carried at market value, real estate and mortgages at book value. All but a minor proportion of bond holdings are rated A or better and a high proportion are obligations of the U. S. Government.

REMARKS:

The experience of Oberlin College to the end of 1946 was principally one of experimental operation. As a guide to judgment, the plan is reported to have been extremely helpful. Substantial profits were realized during 1944, 1945 and 1946. Although the plan did not call for stock purchases above the 150 level, stocks were re-accumulated during the latter months of 1946 at prices considerably under what they had previously been sold for.

## A PLAN BASED ON AN EARNINGS PROJECTION

FUND TO WHICH APPLIED: Various accounts connected with Oglebay Norton & Co., Cleveland, Ohio.

DATE PLAN ADOPTED: 1938.

APPROXIMATE SIZE OF FUND: Accounts total between $5,000,000 and $10,000,000.

GENERAL TYPE OF PLAN: Variable stock-bond ratio. Median is determined by an estimate of future common stock earnings and bond yields.

WORKING DETAILS:

*Median Line*—"Average conditions" are assumed to be the point at which average earnings on common stocks are $1\frac{2}{3}\%$ times the yield on long-term high-grade bonds; this point is the median and a 50–50 division between stocks and bonds is made.

To illustrate, in 1938 it was assumed that $7.50 represented the long-term earnings on the Dow-Jones industrial average and 3% the long-term bond yield. The earnings yield on stocks at $1\frac{2}{3}$ times the bond yield was 5%; therefore 150 in the industrial average (the level at which $7.50 is a 5% yield) provided "average conditions" and was taken as the median.

This earnings projection was reduced to $6.75 in 1940, then restored to $7.50 in late 1943. Shortly afterward, the interest rate projection was reduced from 3% to $2\frac{1}{2}\%$, which gave a median of 180, still in use in 1947.

The earnings projection is simply a "conservative estimate of long-term average earnings based on present estimates of the economic trend." It is obtained in part by long-term estimates of earnings for the individual companies which comprise the Dow-Jones industrial average.

*Buying and Selling Points*—These are at intervals of approximately 25% above and 20% below the median, and a maximum and minimum stock position of 85% and 15% respectively are contemplated. The first substantial sale in a rising market is made at the median; the first substantial purchase in a declining market is made at the first point below the median. This is not considered an inflexible rule, however.

REMARKS:

This plan clearly has a strong element of forecasting in it. At the same time, it serves as an effective "emotion control" and the actual results of operation under it during more than eight years have been extremely good. Stocks were sold in late 1938, purchased moderately in the Spring of 1939, sold at the 150 level again in 1939, bought at the 110–115 level in May, 1940, sold in the Fall of 1940, bought again in late 1941 and early 1942, and sold in 1943 and 1946 at an average realization of about 180. For the seven years prior to 1947 an improvement of about 70% over the gain in the industrial average was achieved, but this included the results of security selection as well as the timing of stock purchases and sales.

A manager of the fund makes this comment on the plan: "As a matter of philosophy we would be more surprised than anyone else if our long term projections proved exact. We believe the value lies in emphasizing perspective and bringing into bold relief the great hazard one assumes in investment management."

## SEVEN STEP FORMULA PLAN

FUND TO WHICH APPLIED: Originated by The Keystone Company, 50 Congress Street, Boston, Mass., for use by shareholders of the Keystone Custodian Funds.

GENERAL TYPE OF PLAN: Variable stock-bond ratio, based upon level of Dow-Jones industrial average. The "zone" method is followed (see Chapter XIII) and a median zone takes the place of the more usual median line. Both the median and the buying and selling schedule are determined by a 50-year trend projection.

WORKING DETAILS:

1. *Long-range Channel*—This is determined by drawing on a logarithmic chart of the Dow-Jones industrials a straight line through the approximate bottom of the bear markets since

1897 and another straight line through the approximate tops of the bull markets since 1897, in both cases ignoring the 1929–1932 period. (See Chart 6, page 88).

This broad channel is then divided into five zones which, with the zone above the channel and that below, give the seven zones from which the name of the plan is derived. The middle zone is the median under the plan. Each year the six lines of demarcation between the seven zones are read from the chart and provide the schedule under which the plan operates for that year.

2. *Buying and Selling Schedule*—A 50–50 division between Defensive and Aggressive securities when the market is in the median zone is recommended—with the suggestion that if this ratio is too high for a particular fund, part of the fund be held outside the plan. Three separate schedules are available to show the appropriate division in various zones for plans with 90/10; 80/20; and 70/30 maximum and minimum stock proportions. The "Investment Timetable" under the Seven Step Plan for 1947 is shown on page 134.

The recommendation is that the account be valued regularly at 90-day intervals and whatever action is necessary to bring about the correct proportions for the current zone be taken only at those times. Thus, when the market average changes zones, the ratio of defensive to aggressive securities is changed; if there has been no change in zones, it is simply a matter of restoring the ratio previously in effect.

3. *Half-way Rule*—Whenever the Dow-Jones industrial average declines to such a level that it is in either zones 1 or 2, the maximum aggressive ratio reached is held until such later time as the average rises to above zone 4. Whenever the average rises to such a high level that it is in zones 6 or 7, the maximum defensive ratio reached is held until such later time as the average falls to below zone 4.

This particular rule differs in two respects from the usual

## INVESTMENT TIMETABLE 1947

| ZONE | The Dow-Jones Industrial Average | PLAN 1 % Defensive | PLAN 1 % Aggressive | PLAN 2 % Defensive | PLAN 2 % Aggressive | PLAN 3 % Defensive | PLAN 3 % Aggressive |
|---|---|---|---|---|---|---|---|
| 7 | ↑ 255 | 90/10 | | 80/20 | | 70/30 | |
| 6 | 254 ↕ 222 | 80/20 | | 70/30 | | 65/35 | |
| 5 | 221 ↕ 193 | 65/35 | | 60/40 | | 57/43 | |
| 4 | 192 ↕ 168 | 50/50 | | 50/50 | | 50/50 | |
| 3 | 167 ↕ 146 | 35/65 | | 40/60 | | 43/57 | |
| 2 | 145 ↕ 127 | 20/80 | | 30/70 | | 35/65 | |
| 1 | 126 ↓ | 10/90 | | 20/80 | | 30/70 | |

form of half-way rule. In the first place, it does not apply if the market average has failed to rise or decline a considerable distance from the median. In the second place, the use of a median zone rather than a single line, combined with the provision that the maximum offensive or defensive ratio is maintained until the market average has passed all the way *through* the median zone, has the effect of giving a higher re-adjustment point on the upside than on the downside. To illustrate, assume that within the year 1947 the industrial average reached zone 6, declined to zone 2, and then returned to zone 5. No major addition of stocks would be made on the downside until 167 was reached. On the way up, the first major sale of stocks would not be made until 193 was attained. (In actual practice, the 1946 high was in zone 5, so that a re-adjustment was called for on the first quarterly date the market average closed in zone 4.)

REMARKS:

The hypothetical results of this plan, for the 25 years from 1922 through 1946 as well as for the ten-year period 1937-1946, are shown in Chapter XIV.

## DIVERSIFICATION CONTROL INVESTMENT PLAN

## SHEFFIELD SCIENTIFIC SCHOOL

FUND TO WHICH APPLIED: Endowment Fund of Sheffield Scientific School, New Haven, Conn.

DATE PLAN ADOPTED: September, 1944.

APPROXIMATE SIZE OF FUND: Over $6,000,000.

GENERAL TYPE OF PLAN: Variable stock-bond ratio based upon level of the Dow-Jones industrial average. Provides for median level, above which no purchases of stocks are made and below which no sales of stocks take place.

WORKING DETAILS:

1. *Median Level*—130 is used as the median, with no provision for change incorporated into the plan. Was originally chosen on the basis that it was close to both the mean level of the preceding five years and that of the preceding ten years.

2. *Purchase and Sale Schedule*—The "normal" division between equity type and fixed income securities is 35%-65%. The schedule provides for a maximum equity position of 50% and a minimum of 10%. No purchases are contemplated above the median, and no sales below it. The complete schedule is as follows:

| Zone | Control Point in Dow-Jones Industrial Average# | % Change from Preceding D-J Aver. Level | % of Fund in Equities Adjusted to | % of Fund in Fixed Income Securities Adjusted to |
|---|---|---|---|---|
| Maintaining Zone | 264.00* | +10.0* | 10* | 90* |
| | 240.00 | + 6.6 | 10 | 90 |
| | 225.00 | +10.0 | 19 | 81 |
| Adjustment Zone | 204.56 | +12.0 | 19 | 81 |
| | 182.64 | +12.0 | 23 | 77 |
| | 163.07 | +12.0 | 27 | 73 |
| | 145.60 | +12.0 | 31 | 69 |
| | 130.00 | Median Line | 35 | 65 |
| | 116.22 | −10.6 | 39 | 61 |
| | 103.90 | −10.6 | 43 | 57 |
| | 92.89 | −10.6 | 47 | 53 |
| Maintaining Zone | 83.60 | −10.0 | 47 | 53 |
| | 70.00 | −16.3 | 50 | 50 |
| | 63.00** | −10.0** | 50** | 50** |

*At each successive 10% rise in the average from the 264 level sufficient equities will be sold to reduce their percentage back to 10% of the portfolio.

**At each successive 10% decline in the average from the 63 level sufficient equities will be purchased to restore the percentage back to 50% of the portfolio.

#Closing daily average determines action.

3. *Securities Used and Method of Valuation*—"Fixed income securities" include all bonds not in default of interest and preferred stocks paying their prescribed dividend rate. "Equities and equity type holdings" include all bonds in default of interest, preferred stocks not paying their prescribed dividend rates, and all common stocks. All securities are valued at market.

When an adjustment of funds is called for, it is generally made in round lots "across-the-board" on the equity side, i.e., an approximately equal percentage of the market value of each holding is reduced or increased. In the case of fixed income securities, "it is anticipated that reduction or increase of the percentages therein will be facilitated from a practical standpoint by a selection of blocks of individual holdings to accomplish the purpose rather than an 'across-the-board' procedure."

## THE VASSAR COMMON STOCK CONTROL PLAN

FUND TO WHICH APPLIED: Endowment of Vassar College, Poughkeepsie, New York.

DATE PLAN ADOPTED: 1938.

APPROXIMATE SIZE OF FUND: Plan originally applied to $3,-000,000 fund, or roughly one-third of total Vassar endowment. Subsequently about $2,000,000 added to this fund, increasing to nearly 50% the portion of total endowment to which Plan applied. Remainder of endowment fund is restricted to senior securities, so that a 100% common stock position under the Plan actually represents not more than a 50% stock position for the entire endowment fund.

GENERAL TYPE OF PLAN: Variable stock-bond ratio based upon level of Dow-Jones industrial average. Provides for median level, above which no purchases of stocks are made and below which no sales of stocks take place.

WORKING DETAILS:

1. *Median Level*—Determined annually by Finance Committee. In selecting this level, the Committee is guided by a ten-year moving average of the Dow-Jones industrials but is free to apply Committee's judgment on this point. At the start, a level of 135 was used; this was later lowered to 130, then returned to 135, raised to 140 in 1946 and to 145 at the beginning of 1947.

*Buying and Selling Schedule*—In a declining market a 50-50 stock-bond ratio is effected at the median level. Further stock purchases are made in three approximately equal amounts at successive 10% declines below the median, a 100% stock position being attained after a third 10% decline. No sale of stocks is made until the market average reaches a level 10% above the median; one-third of the stock fund is sold at this level; a second third after another 10% advance; and all remaining stocks are sold after a third 10% advance.

With 145 as the median, the schedule is as follows:

| | Dow-Jones ind. avge. | Division of fund | |
|---|---|---|---|
| | | Stocks | Bonds |
| Selling points on the way up | 160 | 35 | 65 |
| | 176 | 18 | 82 |
| | 194 | 0 | 100 |
| Buying points on the way down | 145 | 50% | 50% |
| | 130 | 65 | 35 |
| | 117 | 82 | 18 |
| | 105 | 100 | 0 |

The first purchase in a declining market is made at the median level. On the way up, no sale is made until the market is 10% above the median.

3. *Securities Used and Method of Valuation*—High grade bonds and preferred stocks, carried at market value, are used for the bond account. The stock portion contains investment-type common stocks which are sufficiently active to be liquidated easily; defaulted bonds and preferred stocks not currently paying regular dividends are included with the common

stocks. When purchases or sales are required, approximately equal amounts are bought or sold right across the list. Purchases and sales are made as soon as is practicable after the industrial average has reached the required level.

REMARKS:

The results of the Vassar Plan, in actual operation, from June, 1938, to December 31, 1946, are shown in Chapter XIV. The plan produced exceptionally good results during its first five or six years of operation when the market fluctuated in a somewhat narrow range above and below the median level. Successive stock sales in 1943, 1944 and 1945 brought the fund to 100% bond position in September, 1945, which was maintained thereafter. While this prevented the fund from deriving much benefit from the later stages of the long advance, it placed the fund in a strong defensive position. The total shrinkage in the market value of the Vassar fund when the market declined from above 210 to about 167 was only 1¼%.

Future results will obviously depend upon the extent of market fluctuations and upon the accuracy with which the annual determination of the median level is made.

## THE YALE PLAN

FUND TO WHICH APPLIED: Endowment Fund of Yale University, New Haven, Conn.

DATE PLAN ADOPTED: 1938.

APPROXIMATE SIZE OF FUND: Over $85,000,000.

GENERAL TYPE OF PLAN: Constant stock-bond ratio, but with one ratio for a rising market and a different ratio for a declining market. Action is determined by changes in the market value of holdings, rather than by level of any stock price index.

WORKING DETAILS:

1. *Stock-Bond Ratio*—The "normal" stock-bond ratio is 30%—70%. In a rising stock market, the ratio of stocks to the total fund is permitted to rise to 40% and then reduced

to 35% by making sufficient sales of stocks and purchases of bonds. In a declining market, no purchases of stocks are made until the ratio drops to 20% of the total fund. When this occurs, bonds are sold and stocks bought to bring the ratio up to 25%. The 25–75 stock-bond ratio is maintained by making additional purchases of stocks if the ratio drops to 20–80. No sales are made of the stocks bought until the stock-bond ratio reaches 40–60.

2. *Securities Used and Method of Valuation*—High-grade bonds and preferred stocks constitute the fixed-income portion. Bonds are carried at par value for purposes of the plan, preferred stocks at market value. The long list of common stocks held is comprised of investment-type issues which are readily marketable. Defaulted bonds and preferred stocks paying no dividends are classified with common stocks as equities and all are carried at market values. Sales or purchases required by the plan are made proportionately "across-the-board."

When new money is received, it is added at the ratio prevailing at the time of its receipt.

REMARKS:

Broad market fluctuations are required to make the Yale Plan effective. Assuming no change in fixed-income portion, an advance in market value of stocks of about 23% is required to change a stock proportion of 35% to one of 40%. To reduce a 35% stock position to 20% of the total fund, a stock decline of 53% is required. And to raise a 25% stock ratio to 40% takes a 100% advance in prices.

Since the Yale Plan was instituted, only one change has been called for—a cut-back in stocks from 40% to 35% around the 1938 highs. A second reduction in stocks was narrowly missed in 1946.

For Yale's particular objectives—income and capital conservation—the plan is reported to have been extremely helpful.

# PART IV

# DOLLAR AVERAGING

## CHAPTER XV

### How and Why Dollar Averaging Works

So far this book has dealt primarily with the problems of the investor who already has an accumulated sum of capital—whether it be $10,000 or $100,000,000—and whose chief concern is to make it work for him without unnecessary risk of loss. In the strict sense of the word, formula planning applies only to this type of investor.

But there are also a great many investors who are currently building up their investment capital. They have an excess of current income which they wish to invest in securities in a small way as they go along; their current additions to their investment fund are large in relation to the amount which they have already invested and their primary problem is to keep from always buying common stocks or similar securities when they are too high in price to be good investments.

There is a method of systematic investing which is ideal for this type of investor. Known as "Dollar Averaging," it is the simplest form of investment plan. The "formula" is nothing more than the regular purchase of securities in equal dollar amounts, but the potential results from strict adherence to such a program are startling.

No one needs to be told that the same amount of money will buy a greater number of shares of any stock when the price is low than it will when the price is high. This very obvious fact, however, is the explanation of the successful working of Dollar Averaging.

The idea is to invest at some regular time interval, regardless of the level of prices, a fixed amount of money, such as $100 on the first of every month or $500 at three months' intervals. Any amount of money and any time interval can be used; the important part is to stick to the schedule, no matter how low or how high the market goes. The lower prices go, the greater will be the number of shares purchased with the fixed sum, and the lower will be the average cost of all shares purchased. And the higher prices go, the fewer shares will be obtained.

Over a long period of time, the result will be that, impossible as it may seem, the average *cost* of all shares purchased will be lower than the average *price* at which the shares were bought. A simple example will illustrate the point: Assume that $1,000 is to be invested at some regular interval in the shares of a certain stock, and that the first two purchases are made at prices of 100 and 80. This is the way it would work:

| Price | Shares purchased each time | Total shares purchased | Average price | Average cost of shares purchased |
|---|---|---|---|---|
| 100 | 10 | 10 | 100 | 100 |
| 80 | 12.5 | 22.5 | 90 | 88.89 |

The average *cost* of 88.89, of course, is obtained by dividing the total amount invested, $2,000, by the total number of shares purchased; and the reason it is lower than the average *price* is that more shares are bought at 80 than at 100.

Now assume that the same procedure is continued and that six more purchases of this same stock are made, at prices down to 20 and then back up as far as 80. This is the way the entire program would then look:

| | Price | Shares purchased each time | Total no. shares held | Total amount invested | Current value of investment |
|---|---|---|---|---|---|
| 1st purchase | 100 | 10 | 10 | $1,000 | $1,000 |
| 2nd purchase | 80 | 12.5 | 22.5 | 2,000 | 1,800 |
| 3rd purchase | 60 | 16.7 | 39.2 | 3,000 | 2,352 |
| 4th purchase | 40 | 25 | 64.2 | 4,000 | 2,568 |
| 5th purchase | 20 | 50. | 114.2 | 5,000 | 2,284 |
| 6th purchase | 40 | 25 | 139.2 | 6,000 | 5,568 |
| 7th purchase | 60 | 16.7 | 155.9 | 7,000 | 9,354 |
| 8th purchase | 80 | 12.5 | 168.4 | 8,000 | 13,472 |

Now if the price of the stock goes back to 100, but no more purchases are made, the value of the investment will be $16,840.

Because the purchases were made in a declining market, a loss is shown right from the start, and at the low price, which prevailed when the fifth purchase was made, the loss is greater than 50%. Note, however, that the price of the stock had to advance only to 43 to recover the entire loss, and from then on profits mounted rapidly. The average *price* paid over the course of this program was 60; the average *cost* of the 168.4 shares held was less than 48.

The starting point for a program of this type makes comparatively little difference. Actually, a bull market peak is nearly as good a time as any to begin, since few shares will be bought at the high prices anyway. If in the example above we had assumed 60 as the starting point, with the market rising to 100, declining to 20, and finally returning to the 60 level, and if we had assumed purchases made at the same levels as those given, the average price and the average cost would not have been changed. At the return to the starting point of 60, however, the current value of the $8,000 investment would have been $10,164. If no further purchases were made, and the price went on up to 100, the value would become the same as in the first example, namely, $16,840.

The wider the fluctuations in price, the better an "averaging" program will work—provided, of course, that prices eventually recover from their lows. The examples given are pretty extreme, a decline of 80% and a subsequent rise of 400% being a rather rare occurrence in the stock market. (That is just about what the Dow-Jones industrial average did between 1929 and 1937, however, except that the 1929–1932 decline was closer to 90% and the subsequent recovery went only half way back to the 1929 high.)

A convenient way to test the results of Dollar Averaging is to use the Dow-Jones industrial average for a number of periods in the past. In Table 10, therefore, are shown the results of Dollar

TABLE 10

DOLLAR AVERAGING IN THE DOW-JONES INDUSTRIAL AVERAGE

RESULTS OF INVESTING $100 A MONTH OVER TEN-YEAR PERIODS ENDED FROM 1937 TO 1946

| 10 Years ended December 31 | Shares Bought | Average Price | Average Cost | Total Cost | Market Value at end of 10 years |
|---|---|---|---|---|---|
| 1946 | 85.91 | 144.25 | 139.68 | $12,000 | $15,223 |
| 1945 | 87.14 | 141.11 | 137.71 | 12,000 | 16,810 |
| 1944 | 90.28 | 136.04 | 132.92 | 12,000 | 13,751 |
| 1943 | 94.18 | 131.54 | 127.41 | 12,000 | 12,798 |
| 1942 | 100.96 | 126.19 | 118.86 | 12,000 | 12,055 |
| 1941 | 109.12 | 121.96 | 109.97 | 12,000 | 12,108 |
| 1940 | 108.30 | 123.75 | 110.80 | 12,000 | 14,201 |
| 1939 | 104.49 | 134.36 | 114.84 | 12,000 | 15,699 |
| 1938 | 99.85 | 151.67 | 120.18 | 12,000 | 15,423 |
| 1937 | 95.90 | 161.11 | 125.13 | 12,000 | 11,590 |

Averaging as applied to this index of 30 industrial stocks over the ten ten-year periods which ended with each year from 1937 to 1946. The earliest period started on January 1, 1928, and the most recent one on January 1, 1937. A Dollar Averaging program need not continue for ten years, this period being used simply as an initial test.

For these examples, a $100 investment in the average at the beginning of each month was assumed. A total investment of $12,000, therefore, would have been made during each ten-year period. No allowances were made for brokerage fees, odd-lot differentials, or income. Also, to make the calculations simpler, it was assumed that it is possible to purchase fractional shares of the average, which of course cannot be done in actual practice. (A subsequent example, however, will show that minor variations in the amount invested each time do not in the long run detract from the result.)

The results at the end of ten years' purchases vary, it can be seen, from a $410 decline from cost, in the program ended in 1937, to a $4,810 profit in that ended December, 1945. On average, the profit on the original investment amounted to around 16% when the program ended. But obviously, the level of the market at the end of the purchasing period has a considerable effect upon the immediate result. At the 1937 year-end the Dow-Jones average stood at 120.85; it closed the year 1945 at 192.91.

A second and perhaps more enlightening test is to ascertain the length of time it would have taken to achieve a certain percentage profit on the money invested. The same assumptions are made as in Table 10, but no time limit is set on the program. Instead, the program is assumed to have ended on the first date when all previous purchases could have been liquidated at an average profit over cost of 40%. Table 11 shows the length of time this would have taken for programs started at the beginning of each year since 1928.

TABLE 11

LENGTH OF TIME REQUIRED TO ACHIEVE 40% PROFIT ON MONTHLY DOLLAR AVERAGING PROGRAMS IN DOW-JONES INDUSTRIAL AVERAGE STARTED JANUARY 1 EACH YEAR 1928–1943

| Date Program Started Jan. 1 | Time Required to Achieve 40% Profit |
|---|---|
| 1928 | 1 year, 2 months |
| 1929 | 7 years, 4 months |
| 1930 | 5 years, 11 months |
| 1931 | 4 years, 8 months |
| 1932 | 1 year, 6 months |
| 1933 | 1 year, 2 months |
| 1934 | 2 years, 3 months |
| 1935 | 2 years, 3 months |
| 1936 | 10 years, 0 months |
| 1937 | 9 years, 0 months |
| 1938 | 7 years, 10 months |
| 1939 | 6 years, 10 months |
| 1940 | 5 years, 9 months |
| 1941 | 4 years, 9 months |
| 1942 | 3 years, 9 months |
| 1943 | 3 years, 5 months |

Every program started between January 1, 1928, and January 1, 1943, would have been completed by the end of 1946 on this basis and in only one case (starting January 1, 1936) would the full ten years have been required. Programs begun at the start of 1944, 1945 or 1946 would not have achieved a 40% gain before the market turned down in 1946.

The advantage of investing the same number of dollars each time, instead of buying an equal number of shares each time, can be seen by comparing the "average price" and "average cost" figures shown in Table 10, as they would actually have worked in terms of the industrial average. Thus, if an investor had bought one share of the average the first of each month for the ten years ended December 31, 1946, he would have found at the end of the period that the average *price* he had paid was 144.25; by investing, instead, $100 in the average at the start of each month, he would have found at the end of 1946 that his average *cost* had been only 139.68.

A comparison of average prices and costs shown in the table for the various periods illustrates the statement previously made that the wider the price fluctuations, the better the result is apt to be. Since about 1933, fluctuations in the Dow-Jones average have been relatively moderate compared with those in the preceding six years. The differences between average price and average cost, accordingly, are considerably less pronounced in the four most recent programs than in the six preceding ones. This point has a bearing on the choice of securities for use in a Dollar Averaging program, to be discussed in a subsequent chapter.

However, the primary reason for adopting some sort of plan does not lie merely in the advantage of Dollar Averaging over buying the same number of shares of stock at regular intervals. Even the latter program is for many investors apt to be more satisfactory in the end than "hit-or-miss" buying—that is, accumulating funds and investing them only at times when it "seems like a good idea."

The results shown need to be measured against what investors actually did during this time. The investor who resisted the temptation to buy too early on the way down in 1930 and 1931, had the courage to buy in 1932, the sense to sell in 1936 or 1937 and to buy in 1942 probably need not consider Dollar Averaging—or any other formula plan. For others, especially those currently in the position of accumulating their investment funds out of savings from regular income, a consideration of the practical aspects of applying Dollar Averaging is warranted.

# CHAPTER XVI

## SPACING OF PURCHASES IN "DOLLAR AVERAGING"

FROM the practical investment standpoint of applying Dollar Averaging to real money, there are a number of important questions to be answered. One is: Is it necessary to invest as frequently as once a month, or will a less frequent interval do as well?

This question is important, especially if the amount of money to be invested in this way is limited. If approximately as good results can be obtained by accumulating funds for six months or a year and investing all at one time, it should be cheaper to do it this way, since purchasing costs may be disproportionate on small amounts. It also helps solve the problem of dividing the amount to be invested into even numbers of shares.

The answer appears to be that in the long run it makes little difference and such differences as do exist are largely a matter of chance. When prices are advancing, it is better to spread purchases out than to make them only at the end of six months or a year, but the opposite is true when prices are falling.

This is illustrated in Table 12,which reduces to the comparable figures of average cost (in terms of the Dow-Jones industrial average) four methods of Dollar Averaging for ten periods ended December 31, 1946, varying in length from one year to ten. The assumed dates of purchase for the four methods are the first day of each month, the first day of the final month in each three and sixth month period, and December 1 each year.

The most striking variation shown is for the single year 1946, which demonstrates the short-term importance of pure luck. On a straight monthly basis, the average cost of purchases made from January 1 to December 1 was 191. Waiting for the first

TABLE 12

MONTHLY VS. QUARTERLY, SEMI-ANNUAL AND ANNUAL SCHEDULES

COMPARISON OF AVERAGE COSTS OBTAINED BY PURCHASING INDUSTRIAL AVERAGE ONCE, TWICE, FOUR OR 12 TIMES A YEAR

| | Average Cost | | | |
|---|---|---|---|---|
| Periods ended Dec. 31, 1946 | Monthly purchases | Quarterly purchases | Semi-annual purchases | Annual purchases |
| One year ...... | 191 | 185 | 187 | 168 |
| Two years ..... | 178 | 178 | 183 | 179 |
| Three years .... | 164 | 164 | 168 | 167 |
| Four years ..... | 156 | 156 | 159 | 156 |
| Five years .... | 142 | 143 | 145 | 145 |
| Six years ...... | 139 | 138 | 139 | 139 |
| Seven years .... | 138 | 137 | 134 | 138 |
| Eight years .... | 138 | 138 | 135 | 139 |
| Nine years ..... | 137 | 137 | 134 | 140 |
| Ten years ..... | 140 | 138 | 135 | 138 |

day of March, June, September and December resulted in the appreciably lower average cost of 185. But waiting for six months, to June 1 and December 1, led to the somewhat higher cost of 187, because on June 1, 1946, the average happened to be close to its high for the year. Best of all was the result of waiting all year, until December 1, when the purchase date would have coincided with one of the lowest levels of 1946 and given a cost of 167.50.

But in none of the longer periods is there any such extreme variation and there is little apparent consistency in favor of any particular interval. So one appears safe in concluding that anyone who is determined to follow a Dollar Averaging program long enough to insure its working at all, might as well be guided by his own convenience or preference in deciding how frequently to make his purchases.

The amount of money available for investment and the type of security chosen to effect the program will naturally be important factors, since these determine the cost of making purchases. The minimum Stock Exchange commission at the time this is written is $5. At various price levels, this means that to secure the most economical result, the following amounts must be invested in one stock at one time:

| Price per Share | Amount |
|---|---|
| $10 | $330 |
| 20 | 560 |
| 30 | 720 |
| 40 | 880 |
| 50 | 1,000 |

Leaving aside for the moment the question of diversification in a Dollar Averaging program, the possible use of open-end investment company shares, for the sake of convenience and economy, might be considered. (See Chapter V for a more complete description of investment companies.) Sold at a standard "selling charge" or "load" ranging from about $6\frac{1}{2}$% to $8\frac{3}{4}$% in most cases (except on amounts over $25,000), investment company shares can usually be bought in small amounts at no increase in proportionate cost.

In comparison, $100 can only be invested in a listed common stock at an expense (simply for minimum commission and odd-lot fee) ranging upward from 5%, depending on the price. The lower the price, the more significant the odd-lot fee. With only $50, the commission cost is virtually prohibitive. While commissions at time of sale are proportionately much lower, because presumably a larger amount of stock will be involved, they are not to be ignored. On the other hand, most investment companies redeem shares at or very close to liquidating value.

Some investment companies have no minimum number of shares which can be purchased; others do but provide that the minimum applies only to initial purchases. A few investment companies have adopted plans for facilitating Dollar Averaging programs which are purely voluntary on the part of the investor and incur no extra cost.

There are also in existence a number of companies identified by the Investment Company Act as "periodic payment plans." These provide usually for a fixed ten-year program, including the re-investment of dividends and frequently carrying, as an optional feature, life insurance to the amount of the unpaid portion. They can usually be obtained in amounts as low as $10 a month (after a required initial payment of $20), and the investor can count on reminders from the company if he is lax in his payments. Fractional shares can be purchased in this way, insuring complete investment of the entire payment each month.

Selling and administrative costs on such plans are apt to be relatively high. While it has proved possible in some cases to reduce over-all charges to a basis nearly comparable with equal purchases of the same securities without the "plan," heavy deductions must be made in the early years. Thus, if the investor is unable to continue for the full period provided, his average expense is bound to be high.

Otherwise, such plans are an especially convenient way to follow a Dollar Averaging program, and the automatic re-investment of dividends, which produces a compounding of income, will, in addition, result in a more rapid growth of capital.

## CHAPTER XVII

### Volatility—More Profits, Greater Risks

Dollar Averaging can be applied to any kind of security an investor wants to accumulate—from bonds which fluctuate only moderately down to the most radically speculative common stocks. The simple mathematical principle involved holds true provided only that there is *some* fluctuation in price.

From here on, however, the type of securities chosen for a Dollar Averaging program can make an enormous difference in the results to be expected. Most significant of all is the volatility of the securities used—that is, the rate at which they advance in rising markets and decline in falling ones. The faster a stock moves, in both directions, the better will be the end result, assuming that the end is not reached before sufficient recovery from the bottom has been attained.

Choosing securities solely on the basis of volatility entails obvious dangers and disadvantages. Losses are greater in the declining phases, income is apt to be lower and less certain, and the danger of insufficient recovery is greater. But the probable long-term capital growth from a Dollar Averaging program varies so much in proportion to the volatility of the securities used that the subject deserves consideration even by fairly conservative investors.

The reason wide fluctuations in the stocks used make so much difference is simple: more shares are bought at low prices than at high in any Dollar Averaging program. Therefore, the greater the difference between the low and the high prices, the greater the opportunity for the principle to work most effectively. Comparative results for the Dow-Jones industrials in periods of wide and relatively narrow fluctuations have already illustrated the same effect.

The majority of individual securities tend to move up and down faster than a market average made up of "blue chips" and other active market leaders. This is normally true to some extent of many reasonably conservative issues and, of course, applies in the extreme to a great many of the lower-priced and more speculative shares. The investor has a wide range from which to choose and can decide for himself where he had best compromise between volatility and risk.

To show the effects of using different types of securities in a Dollar Averaging program, a series of three indexes were used. They are the same as those used in Part II and are fully described in Chapter VII. The Fully Managed Stock Fund is included in order to compare the relative effects on a Dollar Averaging program of straight volatility and of superior selection or investment management within the portfolio of securities used.

The period of the comparison is January 1, 1937, through December 31, 1946. The industrial average stood at almost identical levels on the two dates and the volatility indexes have been adjusted so that they, too, show neither gain nor loss for the ten years. The Fully Managed Stock Fund, which is unadjusted, was about 32% higher at the end than at the beginning. (Dividends were ignored in all cases.)

Quarterly purchases were assumed, the amount invested each time being $250. A total of $10,000, therefore, was hypothetically invested in each program, from January 1, 1937, through October 1, 1946. Total market value is shown as of the close, December 31, 1946. (See Table 13).

Total market values at the end of the ten years, it can be observed, are higher than cost in almost perfect proportion to the relative volatilities of the securities used. Thus, the program using the industrial average shows a profit of 27%; that using Business Cycle Stocks 49%, Low-Priced Stocks 80% and Highly Speculative Stocks 148%.

The risks of loss were also roughly equal to the differences in volatility. At the 1938 low, which occurred when only five quarterly investments had been made, a Dollar Averaging program in the industrial average would have been worth 37½% less than the amount invested. In comparison, programs using the more volatile issues would have shown losses of 47%, 62% and 63% respectively.

All four indexes dropped to equally low or lower levels at about the half-way point of the ten-year period; the Dollar Averaging programs, however, show considerably smaller percentage losses at this point than on the earlier date. It is clear that the large number of purchases made in the meantime at relatively low prices had already reduced the average cost of shares held well below that obtained prior to March 31, 1938.

Some answers to the question of "growth" or "management" vs. volatility alone are provided by a comparison of the results for the Fully Managed Stock Fund with those of the other programs. In over-all result at the end of ten years, the program using this well-managed investment company falls somewhat below that of the program using Low-Priced Stocks and well below that using Highly Speculative Stocks. It had, however, incurred a smaller loss at the March 31, 1938, low than any of the other programs except that using the industrial average, and at the 1942 low its decline from cost was the smallest of all.

TABLE 13

EFFECT OF VOLATILITY ON DOLLAR AVERAGING RESULTS

Comparison of Final Market Values and Risk Factors in Programs Using Issues that Differ in Rates of Price Change.* Based upon Quarterly Purchases with $250, 1937–1946.

| Index | Total Amount Invested | Market Value Dec. 31, '46 | % Loss Mar. 31, '38 (after $1,250 invested) | % Loss at 1942 low price (approx. $5,000 invested) |
|---|---|---|---|---|
| Dow-Jones Ind. Aver. | $10,000 | $12,700 | 37½% | 27% |
| Business Cycle Stocks | 10,000 | 14,886 | 47 | 28 |
| Low-Priced Stocks | 10,000 | 17,969 | 62 | 37 |
| Highly Speculative Stocks | 10,000 | 24,798 | 63 | 40 |
| Fully Managed Stock Fund | 10,000 | 16,804 | 40 | 19 |

*See Chapter VII, pages 44-46, for explanation of indexes used.

Assuming approximately equal volatility, therefore, there is no question that "growth stocks" or a well-managed portfolio of stocks will provide better results throughout the duration of a Dollar Averaging program; the end result is better and the risks diminished. Either the best possible selection of individual issues for their long-term "growth" qualities, or the use of carefully selected management investment company shares is the obvious answer to the question of type of issues to be used for a conservative Dollar Averaging program. Volatility should be given secondary consideration, though not ignored.

For the more speculatively-inclined, volatility can be given more weight. But the following questions warrant careful consideration before deciding to let volatility alone be the determining factor.

1. Is there strong likelihood the program can be continued throughout a bear market?

The superior results of programs using fast-moving issues are almost entirely the result of the large number of shares bought at very depressed prices. If less new money for investment, or none at all, had been available at those times, nothing like the results shown would have been obtained. While any Dollar Averaging program virtually requires investment at all stages of the market, the effects of skipping a few purchases would be less significant in the slower-moving issues.

2. Of perhaps greater importance, *will* the program be continued throughout a bear market?

To continue buying more shares regularly when substantial losses already exist and are increasing requires both will power and faith in the ultimate effectiveness of the Dollar Averaging idea.

3. Can the securities used be counted upon to move with the market, but faster, at all times?

This is the same question which faces the investor with an accumulated fund who is following a formula plan, and is discussed in detail in Chapter V. The conclusion that the use of certain types of investment company shares is practically essential in a plan stressing capital gains through volatile stocks is equally applicable to a Dollar Averaging program.

## CHAPTER XVIII

### TECHNICAL VARIATIONS

ONCE the underlying idea and merits of Dollar Averaging are understood, a number of additional practical questions usually occur to an investor. For the sake of convenience and simplicity, the most frequent of these have been arranged in two groups: In the present chapter technical questions on variations of the basic method are discussed. Other questions, which involve more complicated concepts, are reserved for Chapter XIX.

I. *Is it necessary to confine purchases to a single issue throughout the program in order to make the method "work"?*

Definitely not. Most securities move up and down in price more or less together, so that approximately the same results can be expected from a diversified list, each issue purchased at a different time, as from a single issue, provided that the various issues are all of about the same type, or volatility.

To illustrate this, four individual stocks—all active, listed issues but representing four different industries—were used for a hypothetical program in the 1937–1946 ten-year test period. The stocks were American Car & Foundry, Bethlehem Steel, Chrysler and U. S. Rubber. In this case, semi-annual purchases with $500 were assumed and the purchases were rotated among the four issues in alphabetical order; i.e., $500 was placed in American Car & Foundry January 1, 1937, $500 in Bethlehem Steel July 1, 1937, etc. In all, five purchases of each stock were made, at two-year intervals. For comparative purposes, the result was also computed on the basis of an equal division among all four issues on each purchase date. Here are the results as of December 31, 1946:

| | |
|---|---|
| Gain in fund, purchases rotated | 49% |
| Gain in fund, money divided equally among four issues | $42\frac{3}{4}\%$ |

In other words, in this example, it actually worked appreciably better to buy a different issue each time, repeating only after four purchases had been made, than to spread each purchase over the four issues. The better result can only be considered the result of luck. Under other circumstances, it might have turned out the other way. But the proof is sufficient that a variety of issues can be used, if desired, without disturbing the mathematical basis of Dollar Averaging.

One point, however, is important. The effectiveness of the method *will* be impaired if the investor has a tendency to buy more conservative issues when prices are low, more speculative ones when prices are high. In a Dollar Averaging program, it is better to reverse this procedure, buying better stocks at high prices and the most speculative ones at low prices, *if* the investor can tell when prices are high or low.

II. *Once shares of any particular issue have been bought under this method, must they be held to the end of the program, or can shifts be made prior to that time?*

So long as the sale of one issue and the purchase of another are made at approximately the same time and the two issues are of similar type, there is no reason for not doing so, if desired. But again, care must be taken not to change the quality of the holdings at the wrong time.

In general, it would appear to be desirable to map out a definite program and then stick to it with as few changes as possible. Changes in holdings, or in the issues used for the initial purchases, *can* be made, if necessary, without impairing the effectiveness of Dollar Averaging, but there are dangers in the use of judgment at the time and these very dangers are the principal reason for adopting such a program in the first place.

III. *All the examples assume it is possible to buy fractional shares of any issue, which in practice is impossible except under the "periodic payment plans" (described in Chapter XVII). Doesn't the investment of uneven amounts of money, which is necessary in buying full shares, destroy the effectiveness of Dollar Averaging?*

This factor makes little or no difference, so long as the "small change" is held over to the next purchase date and added to the amount then available. In the long run, the uneven purchases can be expected to average out.

Purely as an example, a program was worked out in the same four stocks used in the answer to Question I. Rotating purchases were again made, but this time it was assumed that only $150 was available at each semi-annual purchase date and that only full shares could be bought. Since Bethlehem Steel and Chrysler are both fairly high-priced stocks and neither American Car & Foundry nor U. S. Rubber very low in price most of the time, this provided an extreme example. It is not intended as a recommended method for the investment of this amount of money.

The full record of this hypothetical program is shown in Table 14. As can be seen, the $3,000 which would have been invested over the ten-year period would have been worth $4,563 at the end of 1946. This is a 52% increase and compares with the 49% increase in the Question I example, which assumed purchase of exactly the same issues on the same dates but assumed that fractional shares could be obtained. Commission and odd-lot expense was, however, ignored in both cases.

IV. *How should dividends on the shares purchased for a Dollar Averaging program be treated?*

That depends entirely upon the individual investor. If he needs to spend the income, the method will work just as well without re-investment of dividends—no attempt has been made in any of the examples given in this book to re-invest ordinary dividends. But if he does not need them and is interested in the most rapid possible growth of his capital, then by all means the dividends should be re-invested, thus compounding income which, over a period of years, will add substantially to the result.

He can either add dividends received to his next purchase amount, or accumulate them for a longer interval if that is more convenient. So long as dividends are re-invested at some *regular* interval, the spacing will make little more difference in the long run than the interval chosen for the basic purchases.

TABLE 14

DOLLAR AVERAGING IN HIGHER-PRICED, FULL SHARES

BASED ON $150 SEMI-ANNUAL PURCHASES, 1937–1946, IN FOUR DIFFERENT COMMON STOCKS

| Date of Purchase | Issue Bought | Price | Shares | Cost | Cash left over* |
|---|---|---|---|---|---|
| 12/31/36 | Amer. Car & Foundry | $59\frac{1}{4}$ | 2 | $118 | $32 |
| 6/30/37 | Bethlehem Steel | 84 | 2 | 168 | 14 |
| 12/31/37 | Chrysler | $47\frac{5}{8}$ | 3 | 143 | 21 |
| 6/30/38 | U. S. Rubber | 36 | 4 | 144 | 27 |
| 12/31/38 | Amer. Car & Foundry | $34\frac{1}{8}$ | 5 | 171 | 6 |
| 6/30/39 | Bethlehem Steel | $51\frac{7}{8}$ | 3 | 156 | — |
| 12/31/39 | Chrysler | $89\frac{1}{2}$ | 1 | 90 | 60 |
| 6/30/40 | U. S. Rubber | $19\frac{1}{2}$ | 10 | 195 | 15 |
| 12/31/40 | Amer. Car & Foundry | $30\frac{3}{8}$ | 5 | 152 | 13 |
| 6/30/41 | Bethlehem Steel | $72\frac{1}{2}$ | 2 | 145 | 18 |
| 12/31/41 | Chrysler | $45\frac{3}{8}$ | 3 | 136 | 32 |
| 6/30/42 | U. S. Rubber | 17 | 10 | 170 | 12 |
| 12/31/42 | Amer. Car & Foundry | $25\frac{3}{4}$ | 6 | 154 | 8 |
| 6/30/43 | Bethlehem Steel | $64\frac{1}{2}$ | 2 | 129 | 29 |
| 12/31/43 | Chrysler | $81\frac{3}{8}$ | 2 | 163 | 16 |
| 6/30/44 | U. S. Rubber | $52\frac{1}{2}$ | 3 | 158 | 8 |
| 12/31/44 | Amer. Car & Foundry | $39\frac{1}{2}$ | 4 | 158 | — |
| 6/30/45 | Bethlehem Steel | $79\frac{3}{8}$ | 1 | 79 | 71 |
| 12/31/45 | Chrysler | $131\frac{1}{8}$ | 1 | 131 | 90 |
| 6/30/46 | U. S. Rubber | $69\frac{1}{2}$ | 3 | 209 | 31 |

*Added to total to be invested at next semi-annual date.

SUMMARY OF RESULTS

| Shares Held | Stock | Price | Dec. 31, 1946 Value |
|---|---|---|---|
| 22 | Amer. Car & Foundry | $49\frac{3}{4}$ | $1,095 |
| 10 | Bethlehem Steel | 91 | 910 |
| 10 | Chrysler | $91\frac{1}{2}$ | 915 |
| 30 | U. S. Rubber | $53\frac{3}{4}$ | 1,612 |
| | Uninvested cash | | 31 |
| | Total Value Dec. 31, 1946 | | 4,563 |
| | Total Investment | | 3,000 |

If investment company shares are used, however, it is important to re-invest "capital gains" distributions, whether or not ordinary dividends are reinvested. Capital gains dividends are not income in the commonly-accepted sense of the word but represent realized profits which, under existing tax laws, investment companies are virtually required to pay out in the year realized. They may be very substantial in certain years, so that failure to re-invest them could easily disturb the automatic working of a Dollar Averaging program. Since they are most apt to be paid in years of relatively high security prices, a case might be made for delaying re-investment, but for most investors immediate re-investment (especially where the investment company makes this possible without cost) would seem to be the most advisable procedure.

V. *Can the Dollar Averaging principle be applied to a non-accumulating fund—i.e., where the investor starts off with, say, $10,000 and does not expect to add new money to it in the future?*

For such a fund, the other "automatic timing" plans, described in the earlier chapters of this book, appear more likely to produce good results than any attempt to follow Dollar Averaging alone. Dollar Averaging is primarily a method of investing for the person who is still accumulating his investment capital. It provides for the "timing" (more accurately, for the elimination of "timing") of security purchases only, and makes no automatic provision for selling.

The only way Dollar Averaging can be applied to a fund of relatively fixed size is by the simple expedient of spreading the purchases over a long period of time. It is necessary, however, to spread the purchases out over a period of a good many years in order to insure a relatively low average cost. During the past twenty years it would not have been safe to plan on investing a fund in this fashion over much less than ten years. While shorter periods would have worked very well at certain times, they would have worked very badly if their start had occurred in the

TABLE 15

COST OF SPREADING FUND PURCHASES OVER FIVE AND TEN-YEAR PERIODS

A—Five-Year Periods Ended Each Year Since 1928

| Years (inclusive) | Av. cost in terms of D-J ind. av. | D-J ind. av. at start of period |
|---|---|---|
| 1942–1946 | 142.0 | 112.77 |
| 1941–1945 | 131.7 | 130.57 |
| 1940–1944 | 127.9 | 151.43 |
| 1939–1943 | 127.8 | 153.64 |
| 1938–1942 | 125.7 | 120.57 |
| 1937–1941 | 138.1 | 178.52 |
| 1936–1940 | 144.4 | 144.13 |
| 1935–1939 | 138.1 | 104.51 |
| 1934–1938 | 126.6 | 100.36 |
| 1933–1937 | 110.4 | 59.29 |
| 1932–1936 | 90.3 | 74.62 |
| 1931–1935 | 89.0 | 169.84 |
| 1930–1934 | 98.1 | 244.20 |
| 1929–1933 | 114.3 | 307.01 |
| 1928–1932 | 144.7 | 203.35 |
| 1927–1931 | 203.7 | 155.16 |
| 1926–1930 | 209.2 | 158.54 |
| 1925–1929 | 178.3 | 121.25 |
| 1924–1928 | 142.0 | 95.65 |

B—Ten-Year Periods Ended Each Year Since 1933

| Years (inclusive) | Av. cost in terms of D-J ind. av. | D-J ind. av. at start of period |
|---|---|---|
| 1937–1946 | 140.0 | 178.52 |
| 1936–1945 | 137.8 | 144.13 |
| 1935–1944 | 132.8 | 104.51 |
| 1934–1943 | 127.3 | 100.36 |
| 1933–1942 | 117.6 | 50.29 |
| 1932–1941 | 109.2 | 74.62 |
| 1931–1940 | 110.1 | 169.84 |
| 1930–1939 | 114.7 | 244.20 |
| 1929–1938 | 120.1 | 307.01 |
| 1928–1937 | 125.2 | 203.35 |
| 1927–1936 | 125.1 | 155.16 |
| 1926–1935 | 124.9 | 158.54 |
| 1925–1934 | 126.5 | 121.25 |
| 1924–1933 | 126.6 | 95.65 |

two or three years of high stock prices preceding the 1929 peak.

This is demonstrated in Table 15, which shows, in terms of the Dow-Jones industrial average, the average costs of spreading common stock purchases over five-year periods and ten-year periods, since 1924. It is assumed that purchases were made four times a year, on the first day of each quarter. For the five-year programs, average costs would have ranged between 89, if started Jan. 1, 1931, and 209, if started Jan. 1, 1926. And in 12 out of the 19 periods the investor would have been better off if he had invested his entire fund right at the start.

For a *ten-year* program during the same period highest average cost would have been 140, for the one started January 1, 1937, while the lowest, for a program started in 1932, would have been slightly over 109. In eight out of the 14 periods the investor would have been better off than if he had invested the entire amount right at the start.

Thus it appears that for the investor who is willing to wait as long as ten years before achieving his complete common stock investment (meanwhile holding the uninvested portion in high-grade bonds or some other medium which provides some income with little risk), the odds are on the side of spreading out his purchases instead of making them all at once. But the margin is not substantial.

# CHAPTER XIX

## MODIFICATIONS OF DOLLAR AVERAGING

SO FAR, all examples of Dollar Averaging have assumed that approximately equal amounts of new money were available for investment at regular intervals over a long period of time. No attempt has been made to improve upon the results of following a strictly automatic buying program, regardless of the market level at the start or subsequent fluctuations.

Simple Dollar Averaging, if continued long enough, is bound to work reasonably well in any kind of market and under many circumstances there is little point in attempting to improve upon the results by complicating the method. But the question of when to bring a program to an end remains unanswered. In addition, for the investor who desires to do so, there are methods by which potential results can be improved.

I. *Is ten years the minimum length of time a Dollar Averaging program must be followed?*

There is no magic significance whatsoever to the use of ten-year periods in computing past results of Dollar Averaging. On average, this is about the shortest period of time in the past which would have been required to allow opportunity for the basic mathematical principle to attain its maximum effectiveness *under all conditions.*

Obviously, there would have been many times when maximum results would have been achieved in shorter periods. As an example, assume that a Dollar Averaging program was started at any time after the 1929 peak and carried through the 1932 lows. An over-all profit would have been reached fairly early in the succeeding bull market and would have been greatest percentagewise at the 1936–1937 highs. Ending the program and liquidating the securities held at any time in the later stages of that rise would have proved far more profitable procedure than continuing it to the end of a ten-year period, at which time security prices were again considerably lower

Without attempting to forecast future prices, there is no way to tell in advance what the ideal length of time will be, but the investor who wishes to look upon Dollar Averaging simply as a method for *buying* securities and to use his own judgment on when they should be *sold* can certainly do so to advantage.

It is important to realize that once securities have been purchased under such a program, their market value will rise and decline with the market in general, just as if they had been bought in any other way. After a program has been in effect for a number of years, the new money being added to it will be small in proportion to the amount already invested and from thereon results will be considerably affected by the course of prices in general.

Regardless of the size of the existing fund, the Dollar Averaging method is still a good way to invest new money as it comes in. But there is a point at which it is better to separate the accumulated fund from the new money; treat the former as a fund of constant size, applying to it, if desired, the type of formula plan described earlier in this book; and start over again with a new Dollar Averaging program for the new money.

How quickly this point is reached depends primarily upon the trends of prices during the period of accumulation. It is difficult to set any rule for this problem because the type of securities used will make considerable difference. With the industrial average used as the stock portion, Table 11 in Chapter XV indicated that 40% was a reasonable profit expectation; once that figure was achieved, the investor might well have converted his accumulated fund into a regular formula plan account. With more volatile stocks, he would have done better to raise his sights and wait for greater appreciation.

II. *Doesn't the level of prices at the start of a Dollar Averaging program mainly determine its degree of success?*

Prices at the beginning of a program make very little difference in comparison with the importance of prices at the end. Starting market levels apply only to the relatively few shares bought at that time, while those at the end affect every share purchased throughout the period of the program.

In actual fact, however, the *stage* of a market cycle at which a program is commenced can make a fair difference, especially in the early years. But this does not alter the fact that for most people it is still better to follow a mechanical purchasing program than simply to buy stocks when a feeling of optimism prevails.

The most desirable time to start a program, of course, is a little above the bottom of a long-term decline, thereby avoiding higher-priced purchases. But any stage of such a decline is nearly as good, since relatively few shares will be obtained at the higher prices anyway and this eliminates any need to decide when prices have become "low enough to buy." Calculations of the average cost obtained in buying the industrial average over long periods all ending on the same date (December 31, 1942) but starting at different stages of the 1929–1932 decline illustrate the point:

| Start of program | Average cost |
|---|---|
| Dec. 31, 1929 | 115.95 |
| Dec. 31, 1930 | 111.22 |
| Dec. 31, 1931 | 109.57 |
| Dec. 31, 1932 | 118.76 |

Note particularly that more was lost by waiting until six months after the bear market ended to start Dollar Averaging than by starting a few months after the 1929 peak.

The least desirable point to start is apt to be about mid-way in a long-term upward movement. This can mean making a good many purchases at high prices, which will delay the achievement of a low average cost. However, when this is the case, profits on purchases accumulate right from the start, and there is nothing to prevent the investor who finds, after two or three years, that existing prices are well above what he has already paid in, from taking his profits and starting a fresh program.

III. *Is there not some mechanical way to avoid partially or entirely making so many purchases at high levels, so as to be able to make more when prices are lower?*

Because Dollar Averaging in itself, if followed faithfully, forces the investor to buy fewer shares at high prices and more at low prices, there is less advantage to striving for this goal than might be imagined. However, it is perfectly possible to adapt a number of the formula plans described in Section II to a Dollar Averaging program and to improve the results thereby.

One method, which is an adaptation of the Constant Ratio plan, is to start by dividing the amount available for investment into two equal portions, with the intention of building up both a stock fund and a cash or high-grade bond fund. Before making each purchase, calculate the current value of both funds. If the stocks are then worth less than 45% of the entire fund, invest the whole amount in stocks. If stocks amount to between 45% and 55% of the total, divide the amount as before between stocks and bonds. If stocks are up to more than 55% of the total, place the entire amount in bonds. (A "gap" between the ratios used in rising and declining markets is necessary to prevent purchases or sales too quickly after a change in trend.)

This method was applied to a hypothetical program in the industrial average for the 1937-1946 period, with quarterly purchases assumed. At the beginning of each three months $300 was invested in the average and $300 placed in a bond fund, except that if stocks had fallen below 45% of the total value, the entire $600 was placed in stocks, and if stocks were above 55% of the total value, the entire $600 was placed in bonds. (The bonds were assumed not to fluctuate at all.)

On 31 of the 40 purchase dates, the method required an equal division of the money. But at the start of 1938, at 120.57, and again on April 1, 1942, at 99.95, the total amount was placed in stocks. No stocks were bought at the following dates and prices: July 1, 1938 (136.53); July 1, 1944 (148.46); July 1, 1945 (165.91); October 1, 1945 (183.37); January 1, 1946 (191.66); April 1, 1946 (199.19) and July 1, 1946 (206.47). Thus, double advantage was taken of two of the lowest levels which occurred during the period, and all stock purchases were avoided after April 1, 1945, and until October 1, 1946, when the stock market had declined sharply.

The result of modifying straight Dollar Averaging in this fashion would have been, at the December 31, 1946, level of 177.70, a gain of 14½% on the total investment of $24,000. If, instead, the amount had been divided evenly each time, the comparable gain would have been about 13%. The small difference naturally imposes a question whether the additional effort would be worth while to many investors.

It should be noted, however, that the 14½% gain on the modified program was accomplished on a total common stock investment of $10,500 (the gain on stock investment alone being 34%), while the simpler program entailed a $12,000 investment in stocks (the gain on stocks alone was 26%). At the end, the modified program held $13,500 in bonds, compared with $12,000 in the simple one, a difference which would bring about a comparison more favorable to the modified program at a lower market level. And if stocks more volatile than the industrial average had been used, the differences would have been considerably greater.

A second method of increasing stock purchases at low levels and reducing them at high is the adoption of a "median" line or level, above which no purchases at all are made. Below this point purchases could be doubled until funds not previously invested were exhausted. This is an adaptation of the Variable Ratio plan for constant-sized funds, described in Chapters X to XIV, and involves the same problem of determining the "median." If this can be selected successfully, results will be considerably improved.

Hindsight is necessarily involved to some extent in computing past results for this type of program, since we now know the range in which the market fluctuated and can not be certain a different "median" would not have been chosen if a program had actually been started at any specific date in the past. For purposes of an example, however, the Oberlin College long-term upward trend line can reasonably be used. Following the methods just suggested and assuming that $300 was available at the start of each quarter from 1937 through 1946, the result at December 31, 1946, would be a holding of stocks worth $13,150 and accumulated cash (no purchases having been made after April 1, 1944) of $3,000. On the $9,000 invested, the gain would be 48%.

*IV. If new money for investment is available in irregular amounts and at irregular intervals, is it possible to take advantage of the Dollar Averaging principle?*

Strictly speaking, Dollar Averaging requires the investment of approximately equal amounts of money at regular intervals. But the experience of most investors has been that in the long run they would have been better off if any new money ultimately intended for the purchase of stocks had been invested at the time it first became available, regardless of the market level, rather than held until it seemed desirable to make purchases.

Since, however, more money is apt to be available just when security prices are high than when they are low, this would seem to be the ideal use for the type of method described in the answer to Question III. In other words, either follow the "median" line principle, or divide the new money into two parts, one to be used in buying stocks, the other placed in bonds or other stable securities. Buy stocks only when the value of existing stock holdings is below some predetermined percentage of the entire fund.

The latter practice has long been followed by many institutional investors, such as insurance companies and endowed institutions, who are continuously but irregularly receiving new money which must be invested.

## SUPPLEMENT

### Indexes Used in Hypothetical Tests

December 31, 1936=100

| | Dow-Jones Ind. Avge. | Business Cycle Stocks | Low-Priced Stocks | Highly Speculative Stocks | Fully Managed Stock Fund |
|---|---|---|---|---|---|
| 12/31/36 | 100.0 | 100.0 | 100.0 | 100.0 | 100.0 |
| 1937 | | | | | |
| 3/31 | 103.5 | 108.2 | 113.6 | 115.0 | 101.0 |
| 6/30 | 94.0 | 93.9 | 100.0 | 91.0 | 89.2 |
| 9/30 | 85.9 | 81.6 | 86.4 | 67.0 | 77.3 |
| 12/31 | 67.1 | 59.2 | 50.0 | 33.0 | 62.1 |
| 1938 | | | | | |
| 3/31 | 54.9 | 44.9 | 31.8 | 24.5 | 50.2 |
| 6/30 | 74.4 | 67.3 | 50.0 | 38.5 | 67.7 |
| 9/30 | 78.5 | 73.5 | 54.5 | 37.5 | 70.9 |
| 12/31 | 86.0 | 81.6 | 66.4 | 40.3 | 79.7 |
| 1939 | | | | | |
| 3/31 | 73.2 | 58.6 | 48.6 | 29.2 | 64.5 |
| 6/30 | 72.5 | 55.1 | 36.4 | 28.5 | 63.7 |
| 9/30 | 84.7 | 78.6 | 60.4 | 37.6 | 77.3 |
| 12/31 | 83.4 | 67.5 | 52.7 | 31.7 | 74.1 |
| 1940 | | | | | |
| 3/31 | 82.2 | 63.1 | 52.7 | 34.1 | 74.1 |
| 6/30 | 67.7 | 56.5 | 37.3 | 24.7 | 59.0 |
| 9/30 | 73.7 | 57.9 | 43.2 | 25.9 | 63.7 |
| 12/31 | 72.8 | 54.5 | 45.0 | 26.2 | 65.3 |
| 1941 | | | | | |
| 3/31 | 68.2 | 53.1 | 40.0 | 25.1 | 62.1 |
| 6/30 | 68.4 | 55.7 | 40.4 | 24.3 | 62.9 |
| 9/30 | 70.4 | 59.8 | 43.2 | 27.0 | 65.3 |
| 12/31 | 61.7 | 48.6 | 32.3 | 21.1 | 56.6 |
| 1942 | | | | | |
| 3/31 | 55.3 | 49.0 | 36.8 | 19.9 | 55.8 |
| 6/30 | 57.4 | 45.7 | 35.0 | 20.9 | 55.0 |
| 9/30 | 60.6 | 52.2 | 38.6 | 23.3 | 62.1 |
| 12/31 | 66.3 | 50.0 | 39.1 | 35.5 | 67.7 |
| 1943 | | | | | |
| 3/31 | 75.9 | 63.3 | 54.1 | 62.9 | 83.7 |
| 6/30 | 79.7 | 67.5 | 66.8 | 65.5 | 90.0 |
| 9/30 | 77.8 | 64.3 | 58.2 | 59.9 | 87.6 |
| 12/31 | 75.5 | 60.8 | 55.9 | 57.0 | 87.6 |
| 1944 | | | | | |
| 3/31 | 77.1 | 65.1 | 62.7 | 59.5 | 91.6 |
| 6/30 | 82.4 | 70.8 | 71.4 | 71.0 | 99.6 |
| 9/30 | 81.5 | 72.6 | 71.4 | 65.2 | 96.4 |
| 12/31 | 84.6 | 79.2 | 78.2 | 77.5 | 105.2 |
| 1945 | | | | | |
| 3/31 | 85.8 | 84.5 | 84.1 | 84.6 | 110.0 |
| 6/30 | 91.8 | 95.3 | 107.3 | 91.0 | 123.5 |
| 9/30 | 100.9 | 103.7 | 111.8 | 101.8 | 133.9 |
| 12/31 | 107.2 | 113.5 | 129.5 | 130.0 | 148.2 |
| 1946 | | | | | |
| 3/31 | 111.0 | 116.7 | 136.4 | 136.0 | 153.8 |
| 6/30 | 114.2 | 123.7 | 145.0 | 137.5 | 157.0 |
| 9/30 | 95.8 | 93.9 | 95.9 | 93.0 | 127.0 |
| 12/31 | 100.0 | 100.0 | 100.0 | 100.0 | 131.5 |

## Recommended Readings

- How to Make a Fortune Today-Starting from Scratch: Nickerson's New Real Estate Guide by William Nickerson

- Scientific Advertising by Claude C. Hopkins

- How I Learned the Secrets of Success in Selling by Frank Bettger

- The General Theory of Employment, Interest, and Money by John Maynard Keynes

- Monetary Policy Alternatives at the Zero Bound: An Empirical Assessment (Finance and Economics Discussion) by Ben S. Bernanke

- You Can Still Make It In The Market by Nicolas Darvas

- The Richest Man in Babylon - Illustrated by George S. Clason

Available at www.snowballpublishing.com

CPSIA information can be obtained
at www.ICGtesting.com
Printed in the USA
LVHW081402200819
628298LV00027B/520/P